What others are saying about this book:

"Omékongo's poetry embodies the definition of 'Sankofa.'" Through his poetry, Omékongo inspires us all to return to our roots in order to have a complete understanding of where we are going as a human race. As he states: 'Those who do not understand their history are doomed to rhyme with it.'"

— **Haile Gerima**
   Film Director, creator of the critically-acclaimed film "*Sankofa*"

"Omékongo expresses himself with a passion that can only be fueled by a deep appreciation for pain and struggle. His work is not for the faint of heart; it is for the peace of truth."

— **Lani Guinier & Antonio Delgado**
   Harvard Law School

"Lovely, beautiful poetry! Absolutely phenomenal! Omékongo's poetry comes alive and relates to all who read."

— **Princesses Ntombi & Mukelile Zulu**
   Zulu Royal Kingdom

"Omékongo refreshes our memories and inculcates consciousness to rise up and turn the tide to liberate our people across the world."

— **Zolani Mkiva**
   Mbongi (official praise poet/singer) *to Nelson Mandela*

"Omékongo…writes about Oppression with such passion, vigor, and rage that his words reignite my own useful anger at tyrants, fascists, and slavers wherever they work their evils."

— **Kay Bourne**
   Arts Editor, Boston Banner/Bay State Banner

To th
Thank
woke!

family,
me

D1530601

Published by
Free Your Mind Publishing
Boston, MA 02131
(202) 251-7746
(202) 889-5056 (fax/orders)
http://www.omekongo.com

Library of Congress Control Number: 2004096180
ISBN: 0-9760056-0-3
SAN: 256-1883

"Opening eyes, one mind at a time"

Acknowledgements

There are many people who made this book possible. I must first start with my parents, Drs. Dibinga wa Said and Ngolela wa Kabongo. My parents taught me what it means to call myself an African and a human being. They taught me that where I am mentally and spiritually will always be more important than where I am physically and economically. They also taught me the lesson of humility and to never believe that my accomplishments make me better than anyone else or vice versa. Among the more important lessons they taught me is to hate evil, not the people who practice it, irrespective of race, religion, or gender.

My siblings have served as extensions of my parents' teachings. They literally saved my life during my most trying times, often without their knowing. To Said, Musau, Muadi, Shaumba, Kabongo, Kamanampata, Simba, and Moumié, I hope that my words and actions continue to make you proud. Thank you also for helping make this a reality. Special thanks also to Taalib and Taalib, Jr. for your constant motivation.

I also must thank the *Blackout Arts Collective* and *Prophets 4 Non-profits*. You have truly aided in my journey of continually honing my ability to poetically communicate with the people. I would also like to thank Josephine Kamara, Nicole Lindsey, Judith Mbuya, and Marsha James for helping to bring my voice to the Motherland. Thanks to Amadou Mbodj for the French translations and to Amiri Baraka, Dennis Brutus, Abiodun Oyewole, Angela Kinamore, Gus Constantine, and Toni Lightfoot for reading my manuscript. Special thanks to Gemal Woods of Park Triangle Productions for the wonderful art that appears all over this book and producing the DVD.

To all of the students I ever taught, know that no one is perfect, but everyone can lead by example. Set your goals high and never look back. As I have always told you, the world is yours. I also must thank all of my extended family members for allowing me to vibe off of your ability to accept me for who I am over the years.

I also must thank Nikki Giovanni and Maya Angelou from the bottom of my heart for being 2 of the main reasons I started writing at a young age. Ms. Giovanni, your comments on this book, nearly 20 years after I was introduced to your work, really tells me that I am on the right path. I thank you, Maya Angelou, Sonia Sanchez, Amiri Baraka, Lucille Clifton, Rita Dove, Haki Madhubuti, The Last Poets, and many others, because one of the main reasons I write is to show you that some of us young folks are indeed listening to you and trying to carry on the torch.

Last and never least, I must thank my wife, Kendra. Kendra, I never knew love before I met you. Over time, I have found that the true key to success in marriage and any relationship is to grow together. When we solidified our bond in high school in 1994, I knew there were good days ahead, however, as a poet, I could not have written a better future than what we have. I thank you for continually pushing me to be my best and for consistently raising the bar on your expectations of me. I am a better man today because of you. I thank you for being you and allowing me to be me. I love you.

Foreword

This book is a celebration of the human spirit and a reminder of its consequences when manipulated for malicious reasoning. This book is my diary. It is the culmination of my life experiences up until this point in my life. More than poetry, this book represents my passion: my passion for people of African descent to understand their past and use it as a tool for self empowerment; and my desire for all of humanity to realize that so much more could be achieved as a people if we would only take the same energy we expend on hate and use that to improve understanding. The goal of humanity is to learn from the innovations of the past in order to create a better future for all; not the elite, the privileged, or even the "chosen" ones, whoever they may be.

The lessons of history have already been written. We are taking life's multiple-choice final exam. Our responses will determine our promotion to prosperity, or our demotion into further disarray, destruction, and demoralization. It is my hope that the words in this confessional will serve as one of your study guides. Choose your answers wisely.

Table of Contents

7

About the Author

Omékongo Dibinga is an activist, educator, spoken word artist, and Founder & CEO of Free Your Mind Publishing. He received his M.A. from The Fletcher School of Law & Diplomacy and B.S. from Georgetown University. He has also studied at Harvard, Princeton, MIT, Morehouse College, and the University of Cheikh Anta Diop in Dakar, Sénégal.

A first generation Congolese-American, Omékongo writes and performs poetry in English, French, and Swahili, and has occasionally used Wolof in his writings. He has released 2 spoken word CDs. The first CD, "A Young Black Man's Anthem: Love, Afrika and Revolution Revisited," won the 2003 Cambridge Poetry Award for "Best CD." His second CD, "Signs of the Time," was released in June 2003.

Omékongo has performed/lectured nationwide, as well as internationally in South Africa, Congo-Kinshasa, Tanzania, France, Cuba, and Canada. His work has appeared on TV and radio from BET to Voice of America in over 30 countries. He has shared the stage with poetry greats such as Sonia Sanchez, Amiri Baraka, Dennis Brutus, The Last Poets, and Askia Touré. He has also shared the stage with hip-hop personalities such as Outkast, Wyclef Jean, Russel Simmons, Reverend Run, Benjamin Chavis, Free, and Cousin Jeff. Omékongo was a member of the 2001 & 2003 Lizard Lounge Slam Team and is a member of the Blackout Arts Collective and Black Scribe Society. His work has been adapted for curricula in primary, secondary and university institutions around the world.

A dedicated activist for over 20 years, Omékongo plans to develop programs that focus on bridge building between young Africans throughout the Diaspora and helping to improve cultural understanding among all races.

AFRICAN ROOTS

Has Anyone Seen My Children?

I had 6 beautiful children
    They were 6 wonderful and beautiful children
They were full of life and vigor, not a care in the world
    I was raising them to be free minds with free bodies
Nothing was to come between myself and my children...
    Or so I thought

One dreadful day I came home,
    And on my front step my first child lie dead
With a gasp loud as the thunder before the impending storm,
    I burst inside my home
Frantically trying to find my other 5 children
    I searched my bedroom, backyard and kitchen
But every room was emptier than my now empty soul

I asked my neighbor he knew nothing,
  I called my mother she knew nothing,
    My cousin, nothing,
      Nobody knew anything!
        Has anyone seen my children?!
          Oh God, what has happened to my children?!

But then,
    As I bent down on my knees to weep and pray,
I saw faint footsteps withering away in the coming storm
    I followed these footprints
To the intersection where the waters kiss the land
    Did my babies drown?
I had taught them all how to swim
    And I had not heard words of any tempestuous tidal waves
That could have swept them away
    But there they were,
The footsteps of my 2nd, 3rd, 4th, 5th, and 6th born,
    And all I was left with was a heart torn
*   *   *   *   *   *   *   *   *

400 years later,
    I received word from a friend

My children are alive!
    Asante Mungu, my children are alive!
My friend told me they had been kidnapped!

He said that one lives in the minority
    Among many who have ripped away his history
They have convinced him that he is no longer strong
    And he is repeatedly reminded of his inferiority
By police batons
    His nickname is "Nigga"
But his first name is African American

My daughter remembers where she came from
    But she is ashamed of me
She now attempts to deny with all her might
    That her hips, hair and culture
Derived from our once humble home
    Her nickname is "Morena"
But her real name is South American

My other son is fighting hard to survive
    But the government of his brother's country,
It is legislatively stripping him of all means of self-sufficiency
    So that rather than sell bananas and sugar cane
To feed his family,
    He sells drugs, that kill other families
His name is West Indian

My other son and daughter are lost
    Somewhere in Asia and Europe
They are rarely heard from
    Though I'm told that my daughter in Asia,
She believes she is the sole survivor of her siblings

My last son,
    Who has held tight to his roots is almost near extinction
His name is the Australian Aborigine

My children were kidnapped and enslaved 400 years ago

And I didn't even know
That child that was killed,
    That was the mind of the African who was left behind
He became a pseudo-European in his homeland
    Yes!
I am Mother Africa and I am dying and alone!
    And it is my firm hope that one day
My children will come home

Because you see,
    Their continental houses are not homes
It is only my home where the heart is
    Yes,
It is also where the horror was
    But it is also where the history is

And, just as all of the governments of your countries
    Have economically realized,
My children,
    Your home is where the future of the world is

I hear that my children have acquired trillions of dollars
    But their dollars are primarily used
To finance their own oppression
    …And I raised them to be free
So I now survive by whatever the leaders
    Of my children's "homelands" decide
Because my own children are not fighting to free me

What keeps me thriving,
    Is the hope that one day my children will come home
Because reuniting at home
    Is the only way they can ever be whole

My children, come home and liberate yourselves
    Come home and liberate me
My children, come home and liberate…WE
    Come home

Love
(written during my first trip to Africa in Sénégal, 1-1-1998)

You told me Africa was savage,
    Barbaric,
        Heathen
It was hard for me to tell,
    If your "Tin-Tin" cartoon characters were Africans,
Or gorillas
                   WHY?
You told me this **entire** continent "knew not the one true God."
              DO YOU?
              HOW?
Oh, I'm sorry, did you say that
    Africans were "violent and animalistic?"
Could you say that a little louder?
    I don't think that Rodney King;
        Or the Tuskegee-Syphilis experiment victims;
           Or Medgar Evers;
              Or Dr. King;
                Or Emmitt Till;
                   Or Abner Louima;
                     Or my **mother** heard you right!
              HMMM...
You call me a "racist,"
    A "militant,"
        A "revolutionary," and of course,
           A "nigger"
           Funny,
I don't seem to remember you ever taking the time
    To get to know me
But since you think you know me so well, let me ask you
    Do you think I was born angry?
Do you think I just decided to feel ostracized
    From American society?
If you believe that, I guess for you,
    The Senegalese were just born speaking French, right?
              THINK

But alas, you refuse to hear me, begging you for a dialogue
    With your American pride (and prejudice),

And with your American love (and hate),
    You nonchalantly told me:
"If you're not happy here, then go back to Africa"

So I did,
    However,
You didn't tell me you had already beaten me here
    I had to find out when I turned on the TV one day
You look better than ever by the way
    Actually,
I'm sure you've **never** looked this good
    I must call my mother and ask if what I see is true because
        I THINK I'M DREAMING

But nevertheless, I am here
    I'll be back in 9 months
I believe that is enough time to be reborn
    And maybe even become open-minded
        CAN WE TALK THEN?

Sonnet #1 (Napenda Afrika Kabisa)

(written on that same sunrise in Sénégal)

I love Mother Africa so, so much
Scorching sun rays, palm trees, beaches so plush
Beautiful is our humble homeland here
I will forever cherish this brief year

After 21 years, I made it back
White lies of "Afrique" could not hold me back
I walk in the cities and the village
Shocked at survival of Satan's pillage

She is once again rebuilding herself
Despite thieves of all kinds, lusting her wealth
Like a mother she satiates their thirst
Still giving her enemies water first

In this world of greed, with kindness she'll rise
While they watch in awe with coveting eyes
*   *   *   *   *   *   *   *   *

Napenda Afrika kabisa
Miangaza ya jua ya nguvu sana, miangazi, mapwani mengi
Nchi ya mababu ni nzuri na ya heshimiwa
Nitakumbuka mwaka huu mfupi kwa milele

Kiisha miaka ishirini na moja nimerudi
Uongo wa wazungu juu ya Afrika, haukuweza kunirundisha nyuma
Ninatembea mjini na vijijini
Nikashangaa kwa uishi wa uwizi wa Shetani

Inanendelea kujijenga
Hata wizi wa kila namna wanaotahamia utajiri wake
Sawa mama anayemaliza nyota yao
Angali anawapatia maadui wake maji

Katika dunia ya utamaa, na utulivu atasimama
Wanapotazama kitambo na tamaa machoni

Justice
(Written before 9-11-2001)

I come from a land
That has been denied freedom by the land of the free

For more than 140 years America,
You and your Belgian cousins
Have committed crimes in my Congo
Like cutting off the hands of my people
For not producing enough rubber for Dunlop
How can one rebuild a nation without hands?

10 million souls perished
Between 1885 and 1910
And America,
You assisted in that genocide
You and Belgium,
Carved out your Congolese pie in 1885
And today,
I **still** can't get a piece of your American pie?

We were your African anus
Being sodomized by Uncle Sam for our resources
All while swallowing the sinful and sinister semen
Of King Leopold's penis

You laughed as the Belgians
Took our wives hostage
To force us to work
How can one rebuild a nation
With no procreation?

When Belgium "granted" us independence,
We had but one college graduate
In the entire country
How can one rebuild a nation
Without education—each one teach none?

17

The blood of my beloved Congolese people
Is on your hands America!
Don't try to deny it!
That red rubber is dripping
From your fangs and fingers

Now you want me to feel compassion
For Columbine?
You want me to feel compassion
For the actions of Timothy McVeigh?

I feel no sympathy for you America!
For you have yet to realize
That when you sow oppression on others
You only reap it on yourself

Since the arrival of you and the Arabs
My people have never known freedom
And you abuse all your freedoms
And now you're angry because all the ravages
You have committed across the world
Are finally returning to your doorstep

Don't be mad at me,
Your brethren,
Or your government

Be mad at God for God is just
And all God is delivering is justice!

...And I Don't Even Know Her Name
(True story)

Did you know I used to be a conspiracy theorist?
Actually,
I'm still a conspiracy theorist
I've conspired about everything
From Klan contraceptive pills in
Kentucky Fried "Chickens,"
To why so many poor children I've taught
Are now on Ridlin

I believe in almost every conspiracy
Designed to assassinate black leaders
From Shaka Zulu to Patrice Lumumba to Dr. King
And up to the present

I also used to opine
About AIDS being a disease,
Created in Western laboratories
To dispose of black people around the world
But then I had to realize
That my theories on conspiracies
Won't change the fact
That my cousin in Mozambique is dying of AIDS
...And I don't even know her name

Thoughts of AIDS
Coming from gays, junkies,
Or Vietnamese Rhesus monkeys
In Western laboratories
Won't help my cousin see her next birthday
Or the birthday of her child

It's insane when I think of those slain in vain
By this disease with "unknown origins"
But of course it's worse now
Because it's closer to home

I often think about my cousin
And how she lost her husband
To the AIDS Grim Reaper
But then I dug deeper

And found out that he died
Because he had to choose
Between money for expensive AIDS drugs
And financial aid to feed his children

So now that he's dead
And they are going hungry,
He must have died in vain
...And I don't even know her name

U.S. drug companies
Won't lower the prices of their medicine
And so now she too waits to die
Impoverished and ashamed
...And I don't even know her name

No more school for her sons
...And I don't even know her name

Her daughter might be raped
By a gang of infected men
In a futile search to cure their pain
...And I don't even know her name

Will her children die too
Because of this damn Western drug game?
...And I don't even know her name
My cousin is dying of AIDS
...And I don't even know her name!

And I know this sounds repetitive
But for my entire life
Her existence in my mind was negative

And so now that she's HIV positive
I feel like I have to make up for lost time
Because there's too much time lost
Before she's tossed
Into that statistical group of Africans
That die from AIDS, malaria, TB,

20

And probably common colds

But since we don't know their names,
And most Americans believe
That all Africans are the same,
Then unless they died from war or famine
Then they must have died from AIDS!

Not old age, not rabies,
Even the babies,
Let them all die
From that disease we call AIDS,

You know that "AIDS"
Some say it means
Acquired **I**mmune **D**eficiency **S**yndrome
But it might as well mean
"**A**fricans **I**mpoverished **D**eath **S**yndrome"
Because no one cares for their names right?
Well wrong!

Because from now on,
I'm gonna sing my cousin's song
And the song of the throngs
Of those who are dying
In numbers so large
That rivers form from tears of the crying
And mounting AIDS deaths
Keep these rivers from ever drying

But I'm gonna stand strong for my cousin
And fight the fight for her and her husband
Because inability to pay exorbitant prices
For name-brand drugs
Means my cousin might die in shame
But at least for this one soul
It won't be in vain
Because by the time you read this testimony
I will have known her name

Her name is not "African statistic #10,000,001"
Or whatever figure
Will get these drug companies more money
And by the way I gotta inform my friends
That joking about AIDS
Never was and still isn't funny

And if they or you ask why,
I will tell them you that my cousin,
Kuishi*,
She is dying of AIDS
And though some of you may not give a damn,
For those of you who care,
Please join me for a moment of silence
For Kuishi's prayer...

*Kuishi – "To live" in Swahili

22

An Orphan's Cry (Hiki Ni Kilio Cha Yatima)

This is an orphan's cry
In Mbuji-Mayi
It's the cry of a child shedding tears
Over a massacred parent
It's the cry of a child watching her mother
Being gang-raped and slaughtered,
While she waits for her turn in horror

This is an orphan's cry
It's the cry of a child wondering
Where he will get his meal the next day
Because there's no parent
To say "It's okay"

It's the cry of the grass being trampled
By 2 battling elephants
It's the cry of a child
Seeing his father assassinated
And exacerbated by the fact
That his older brother would soon follow

It's the cry of a child
Who can't put his hope in the future
Because he cannot envision
A tomorrow without sorrow

This is an orphan's cry!
It's the cry of a child
Knowing he is condemned to death,
Yet still asking "Why?"

It's the cry of a child watching bullets
And not birds fly over his sky
It's the cry of a child seeing her parents
Slaughtered in Mbuji-Mayi

It's the cry of a child knowing,
It will soon be his turn... to die

*   *   *   *   *   *   *   *   *

Hiki ni kilio cha yatima pale Mbuji Mayi

Ni kilio cha mtoto anayetosha machozi

Juu ya mauwaji ya wazazi wake

Ni kilio cha mtoto anayeangalia kundi la wauwaji

Wakibaka mamaye na kiisha wakamchija

Mda anaposubiri mara yake itafika

Hiki ni kilio cha yatima

Ni kilio cha mtoto ana ajaabu bila wapi

Atapata chakula kesho yake Kwani hakuna Mzazi wa

kumuambia ya Kwamba vyote vitakuwa sawa

Ni kilio cha majani yamekanyangiwa

Na tembo mbili inayopigana

Ni kilio cha mtoto anayeona babaye akiuwiwa na akasirisha

Kwani kakaye atafwatapo

Ni kilio cha mtoto asiyetumaini wakati

Ujao kwani hawezi kuona kesho bila uzuni

Hiki ni kilio cha yatima

Ni kilio cha mtoto anayejua ya kama alihukumiwa

Kwa kufa lakini anajiuliza kwa nini?

Ni kilio cha mtoto anayetazama masasi

Na isipo ndege inayoruka pale mbingu yake

Ni kilio cha mtoto anayeona wazazi wake

Wakichijiwa pale Mbuji Mayi

Ni kilio cha mtoto anayejua ya kama

Mara yake ya kufa ni karibu

Everywhere And Nowhere At Once

Congo in our PlayStations

Congo in our cell phones

Congo in our airplanes

Congo in our space shuttles

Congo in our computers

Congo in our furnaces

Congo - everywhere and nowhere at the same time

Because Congo is not in our mind

Welcome To The Congo

(Written in Kinshasa, 2002)

My beloved Congo,
The joke of the African continent
The world's gold, diamond, and coltan mine
Rwanda's concubine

This country of mine,
Poisoned with the swine that is Western policy
Westerners and Asians exploit the riches,
But live behind gated communities
With underpaid Congolese security

So they're closing the door
On fractured Congolese faces with one hand,
While robbing her of her resources with the other
And no province is safe
Because some of our own,
Corrupted Congolese leaders,
Are involved in this race

But even they can't keep pace
In the face of our Rwandan aggressors,
Annexing our spirit
To their sickened, stricken, sinister soul
To such an extent that to now call eastern Congo,
You must dial Rwandan area codes
While they toy with the possibility
Of introducing Rwandan currency in the east

The United Nations talks of peace
Knowing full well
That peace can only be attained
Through violence

Jean Pierre Bemba
Becoming the Congolese Prime Minister
Can only happen through **violence**

Child soldiers,
Fighting in fear

Of retribution on their families,
Join in the spread of **violence**

Raping my mother country,
And spilling her black coltan blood,
Only continues through **VIOLENCE**

But when I talk to you
About Congolese genocide
With Western **compliance**
Your **response** - silence!

I know
Because I used to be just like you,
Sittin' there smilin'
While other folks lie dyin'
Even bought my wife-to-be a diamond
And probably spilled the blood
Of a distant cousin for it
And **chose** to ignore it

But now I've visited Congolese refugee camps
To find that
There's not even any refuge for refugees
Abandoned Congolese mothers and children
Living in tents
Made out of empty rice bags
While lice drags through their hair

And their daughters,
Living in despair,
Start having babies
At 12-years-old
With 50-year-old married men
With no humility
Who pay them $.25
For their virginity
And the possibility of exchange for AIDS
While the World Bank
Gives this absentee father of a government aid

But I'm searching for a cure for both diseases
Because 4,000,000 have died in 4 years

And too many orphans are shedding tears

As they start dying in the street
At 11-years-old
Because even though it's hot on the outside,
Their inner spirits are cold
From walking around starving in a capital city
That barely has paved roads

And eating ½ a meal a day
Can't heal that
Living on less than $1 a month
Won't heal that
And since you only see
Israel and Palestine on the news
Y'all can't feel that!

So I'm hoping that a thousand words
Can be worth a picture
Because this image of the Congo
May not fit your stomach
But it'll fit your fingers with diamonds,
    Your ears with gold,
        Your cell phones with coltan,
            While newly discovered Congolese oil
            Heats your house when it's cold

But y'all **still** don't give a damn
Even when I talk to you
About Congolese with polio,
Walking as if their left knee
Was glued to their left hand

See there may be a cure for measles and malaria
But there's no medicine for misery
In a country being steered
In the wrong direction
With children dying
From all types of infection
And 12-year-old girls condemned to death
Because rich married men,
Don't use protection
And all of their relationships

End in rejection
It's like the entire country's suffering
From a lethal injection

A second genocide in less than 100 years
That's gone without mention
Along with the fact that we've gone 12 years
Without an election
On the Congolese street
Called the "Avenue of the Future,"
…That's where my father was tortured
And nearly died in detention
So you'll have to forgive me
When I say that our future looks bent in
The eyes of the people

And I'm also pissed off because,
They say, "Long live an independent Congo,"
But I don't remember when it ever was

The international community
Correctly condemns Congolese corruption
By questioning where the ministers bought their cars from
But the world's ears become deaf
When I ask where our invaders got their arms from?

This is the Congo damn it!
And ain't none of it funny
Americans who work here
Say it's a great place to make money
Folks with connections from Bush to Bin Laden
Steady robbin' this country of her resources
Through Lebanese liaisons
Living in the land of internationally sanctioned genocide
Where
        Pathetic US
        + Putrid UN policies
        = Pesticide

They're claiming that they've finally brokered peace
But don't let them fool ya
'Cause up 'til today
We're still diggin' up body bags in Bunia

Because their role in the Congo
Supports nothing but **violence**
Our continual purchase of Congolese resources
That never benefit the masses—**compliance**
Possible experiments with untested AIDS drugs
On unsuspecting Congolese—in the name of **science**
Poems like this to wake us all up—a simple act of **defiance**
All I'm asking for my beloved Congolese people—**self-reliance**
But when I ask you to help me heal the hurting heart of Africa,
Your response—**SILENCE**!

God Bless A...A

You African Americans say
    You no longer have anything
In common with Africans

You Africans say
    You no longer have anything
In common with African Americans

Well,
    The more and more I travel
Certain unifying truths
    Begin to unravel

Your youth look at athletes
    And hip-hop artists as their idols

You have schools
    In which disadvantaged children
Suffer from the same, sorry symptom of studying
    With no books

You think that one is uglier
    The darker their looks

You beg the American government
    To provide you with monetary assistance
When this government has neither apologized,
    Nor expressed remorse
For assassinating your Pan-Africanists

You've forgiven Western governments
    For slavery and colonialism
But they have yet to apologize
    Because they only respect your money
But you, they despise

AIDS is one of the leading killers in your community
    Lack of your own history
Being taught in your schools
    Keeps you from ever working towards unity

Your his-story books
    Primarily speak of white advances
In medicine, math, science, and industrialization
    Making your kids believe
They have never contributed to world civilization
    Leading them and you
To look at Bill Clinton as the Messiah
    When he visited your neighborhoods

In the 1960s,
    You cried over the rights
You fought hard to gain
    Now you cry over the rights you've lost

Your children are malnourished

You spend the majority
    Of your insufficient income
On white products
    With fear of investing in your own people

Your belief in Christ,
    Which was re-introduced to you
In a Western bastardized version
    Has become an obstacle to your development
Since you believe your entire destiny
    Lies in the hands
Of a blond-haired, blue-eyed Jesus
    Because you haven't learned to look inside yourself first
And obey your own thirst

Around the world,
    People dance to our music
Until the wee hours of the mornin'
    But I still can't find one distribution company
That in the majority, we ownin'

Your leaders have warned you
    To live together as brothers and sisters
Or perish as fools
    Yet you foolishly believe

That you can win the battle
    By not linking your cause to a world struggle

Whether fathers die in wars over land
    Or wars over drugs
They've left fatherless black boys
    With dreams of being thugs
And babies having babies alone
    Because thugs don't love
They just spread girls' legs
    Like the withered wings of black doves

The *same* media companies
    Show negative images of you to the other
Using pathetic programs
    To play you against one another

Descendants of the creators of civilization,
    You seem to be losing your might
All because you think you have nothing in common
    Now wake the hell up and unite!

Pulse Of The Motherland

They say you can't judge a book by its cover
But it has become appallingly clear
That you can judge an entire continent
By its media coverage

You can color a whole continent dark
With the paint of poorly placed perception
When you rely on the media
To teach you your Africa lessons

Because I come from a continent,
That the world thinks is a country
And to put it bluntly,
We're all HIV positive
Until proven negative
In the eyes of the media

It's like Africa is either one big safari
Or Kalahari with seethin' heathens
With no sense of religion
And home to animals and animism

Because TV renditions of African afflictions
Have created a depiction
Of a land of savages
Where the world's most dreadful diseases
Exceed the law of averages
And since American TV
Only shows the ravages of a select few nations
Most Americans juxtapose the mother of civilization
With phrases like "damnation" and "starvation"
So if we don't control our own images,
We can't expect to see
A true representation of our beauty

Most non-Africans believe that the most
Africa has given to the world
Are phrases like "Hakuna mtata"
And "Asante sana squash banana"
Along with exotic vacations in remote locations

'Cause I've never heard an American TV news station
Even say we're made up of 54 nations

In the eyes of the media,
We're just underdeveloped wannabe Caucasians
Still searching for civilization
If you buy the media's interpretation
Of who we are
But am I taking this too far?

Because to me,
The real problem be the WB, ABC, & NBC
Which are the real WMD:
*Weapons of **M**ind **D**estruction*

Because too many people,
Including many Africans,
See what they see
Through the smart bombs they call TV
And it's not just the newscasts,
It starts at around age 3

Because I grew up
Watching images of Bugs Bunny
Dressed in grass skirts and black face,
Speaking in "African dialects"
And every 10 years,
There's a new version of Tarzan on the TV set

And I don't know about y'all,
But I recall seeing gorillas pass for Africans
In those "Tin-Tin" cartoons
And if you remove
Marvin Martian's helmet from Looney Tunes
He's probably an African illegal alien
Or a fallen, faithless, famine-stricken African child
With his stomach protruded

And it's these convoluted characterizations
That have helped in creating grown-up policy makers
Who partially base their opinions of our homeland
From films such as "Congo,"
"Gorillas in the Mist" and "The Air up There"

And we can't forget "Tears of the Sun,"
Which left too many tears on the sons and daughters of Africa,
Searching for a resplendent representation
Of our native land

But that won't happen until we Africans
Take responsibility for our portrayal
Because the betrayal of our friends
From FOX, CBS, and CNN
Means we will never see-an-end
To caricatures of the continent of human creation
Which has been made to look
Like she's on her deathbed
And ready for cremation

But we will show the world
That our Mother Africa is strong, vibrant and defiant
Because the pulse of nearly a billion people can never die
When WE control what the world sees,
So we must never comply
To pictures painted by pessimists on TV of our homeland
For we,
YOU & ME,
We are the pulse of Mother Africa,
And we will now show the world
How proudly we will stand!

Free Your African Mind!

Free your African mind, my brother
Free your African mind, my sister

Free yourself from those mental chains
That say you're not from that "dark continent"
When ain't no one on the continent darker than you

Realize you have been brainwashed by wicked white men
But your oppression has also been perpetrated
By your own brethren

I know the rapings, castrations, and lynchings were grueling
But the castration of the mind
Has more longevity than a lynching

You're inching further and further away from your motherland
You let them tell you that your slave-inspired slang was Ebonics,
And not a rich African language with English words,
Thus, you were afraid to speak the word

You believed them when they told you Africa was dark
However, you didn't realize
It's because they've tried to steal her sunlight for centuries

From whitening the ancient Egyptian,
To whitening Beethoven,
To whitening Michael Jackson
You've been brainwashed

From slave codes to black codes to Jim Crow
You've been brainwashed

From K-1 to cum laude
You've been brainwashed

You wanna be American,
Though America has decided she no longer needs you
While an entire continent pleads for you to come home
So free your African mind!

Free those naps oppressed under that process
Free those hips from those tight jeans
That only attract negative attention
And suffocate your natural Nilotic curves

Free those brown luscious lips
From ravishing red lipstick

Free your kidneys from sippin' 40s
And sip fresh waters from the Nile basin

Free yourself from feeling you have to step all over your lady
And step with me up Mt. Kilimanjaro

Free your mind and stop trying to "free willy"
Into your co-partner in our fight for liberation

To deny that you're African
Is to deny your place on earth as the first

Why claim to be a nigga and kill over street corners
When you can claim ancient Nubia?
Why claim a country
When you can have a continent?

I speak to all of you in denial
From African Americans to West Indians
To even continental Africans
Malcolm and Marcus **died** trying to free your mind

Accepting your African blood
Turns you into a worldwide majority
And not a national minority
It stretches your history much farther than Mississippi

It explains why you're as beautiful as you are,
Why you worship like no other
And why you can never be defeated
When you stand on the shoulders of God and your ancestors!

ALL OF YOU RISE!

You ghetto prisoners,

Who are really Ghanaian princes rise!
You proud-to-be bitches,
Who are really Burundian princesses rise!
You who think being born on the continent,
Is enough to make you African rise!
Dark-skinned Latinos rise!
Confused Cape Verdeans rise!
Westernized West Indians rise!
Egocentric Euro-Africans rise!
Amnesic Afro-Asians rise!
Almost annihilated Australian Aborigines rise!

Realize being African is a state of mind
And walk with me into that bright African sunrise
And I guarantee that your mind, body, spirit, and nation
Will rise, rise, rise, high as the glistening skies
Just free,
Your almighty,
African,
Mind!

MY LIFE'S POETREE

I Revolt

My name is Omékongo Luhaka wa Dibinga
Wa Yenga Kakese wa Tshintunkasa

My great grandfather,
Tshintunkasa,
He was one of millions of Congolese
Crippled under Belgian colonial rule
And so in 1895 he revolted
And was assassinated

In 1934,
My great grandfather on my paternal grandmother's side,
Chief Misakabu,
He refused to be exiled from his village Bakwadoba
He was later killed in a Luebo prison
After suffering cruel and quite usual punishment

My paternal grandfather,
Yenga Kakese,
He was a church elder
Being haunted by *King's Leopold's Ghost*
During an uprising in 1961,
He decided to revolt by committing suicide
Rather than be captured by his enemies

My father is Dibinga,
A teacher, priest, educator, and liberator
Who could not live with his people being massacred
Under Belgian and Congolese dictatorial rule
So he revolted and was not only tortured in a Zambian prison
By being stretched in four directions,
But was beaten so severely by government agents
That in 1985 he was left for dead,
But luckily only ended up in a coma

My name is Omékongo Luhaka
I was named after a great warrior
Who saved my grandfather's life when he was a child
This warrior was murdered,
But when his attackers tried to lift his body it would not move

So they cut off his arm as proof that he was slain
But he did not die
Days later he rose from his would-be grave
And returned home one-handed to his village
So that he could continue protecting his people

My name is Omékongo
            Luhaka
                Wa Dibinga
                    Wa Yenga Kakese
                        Wa Tshintunkasa

I live in a time where my people
Are being massacred,
        Miseducated,
            And misled
By the educational system,
        The police,
            The government,
                And themselves

And so,
        I too,
            REVOLT

My Name

My name is Amon Ra, Osiris, Menelik, Omékongo, and Reggie
I am the black man eternal
How dare you call me a Nigga?

I have created civilizations
And I have introduced education into this world
I have constructed pyramids
And I have prevailed in your projects

I have walked on the right side of Ma'at,
Created B-pop, Pop, and Hip-Hop,
And in this new millennium
I won't stop 'cause I can't stop

Fool,
I was using gunpowder before you were born
But I used it to worship God, not to make guns
I invented iron before you were plotting pillage in evil's womb
But I used it to fortify and construct castles,
Not to create cannons

How dare you call me a nigga?
How dare you attempt to confine me to a 5-letter prison cell?
Do you think a 5-letter word can define me?
ME who has walked the earth since the dawn of civilization
And unfortunately gave you birth in the process?

I am the father of eternity and the child of destiny
So "Say my name, say my name"
How dare you disregard and disrespect the name
My momma carefully chose for me
After 9 months of contemplating a badge of honor
For her young Shango in the making

I defy all of your attempts to define me!
I refuse to be relegated
To your shallow and senseless stereotypes!

Even my own, brainwashed brethren,
They attempt to define me with such terminology

But I'm not mad
Because history's amnesiacs can never know a great past,
They don't remember they had

But me, I'll twist everything you throw at me
I'll negate the name "nigga"
And become a brand Nubian knight
I'll turn your death sentences into life paragraphs
And I'll turn my dark continent into a lighthouse
That stands as a beacon of hope and salvation for my people

I will never be a nigga!
As a matter of fact,
If you take the true definition of the term "nigga,"
And put it in context with what you have done to me,
You'd realize that you've been the nigga all along—nigga

I'm gonna reverse all of your acts of ignorance
Starting by making sure you know and never forget my name
My name is Malcolm, Martin, Hakim, Amiri, Malik, Richard, José,
Eduardo, and Omékongo
I am the black man eternal
If you MUST call me out of my name
Call me King, Brother, Bwana, Baba, Hak, or Sir
Because my name will *never* be "Nigga!"

My Life Is A Reality Show

Ma vie est une réalité
Donc, on n'a pas besoin de la télé

My life is a reality show
And so I'm suing the creators of **"Survivor"**
For copyright infringement

You see I grew up on the streets of Roxbury
Where too many brothers were getting buried under rocks
For wearing the wrong shoes and socks
In this **"Hard Knocks"** life
Where you could get **"Jacked"** for a wrong stare
Or for not knowing **"What not to wear"**

And too many other brothers
Watched their **"Big Brothers"** get locked
For trying to become **"Joe Millionaire"** on the block
With no chance of **"Jailbreak"**
All for **"The Love of Money"**

Life was like a real life boot camp living in **"Boston 24/7"**
So believe me when I tell you that Bean Town,
It was more than what you would see
Coming out of Harvard and MIT

I'm talking about my **"Real World"**
Where your brethren could get sent to heaven
If they didn't know the **"Road Rules"**
Like if you saw a crime go down
Say you **"Don't Know Jack"**

And if you were the **"Weakest Link"** in a crew,
You might get your wig pushed back
Because it was too easy
For you to get **"Punk'd"**

And that's why this proud African rolled on the solo
And didn't mind being an ordinary **"Joe Schmo,"**
If it meant I could sleep with both eyes closed

But I guess I was spoiled living with both parents
While too many of my peers
Grew up without an African **"American Idol"**
So they got caught up in gangs
Trying to live that **"Fraternity"** & **"Sorority Life"**
And they were too busy being condemned
By mainstream America
Who couldn't realize that these role-model-seeking soldiers
Were just doing **"Anything for Love"**

Because a prepubescent, poor prince,
He didn't care if he was an **"Apprentice"** to a drug dealer
As long as he could get high
Off the pseudo-paternal persona in his **"Simple Life"**
Because ever since **"The Swap"** was made on African shores,
Black folks ain't never been right

And when it came to the sisters,
It was a real **"Battle of the Sexes"**
We treated each other like **"Rivals"**
In this game of survival

So many young, yearning women
Felt destined to live the **"Single Life"**
Because the bad boy **"Bachelors"**
Showed no respect for the beautiful **"Bachelorettes"**
Unless they had a bangin' body

But many sisters did get caught up with brothers
With cash, **"Cribs,"** and a car
So in their vain attempt to create **"Love Stories"**
These **"Dream Chasers"** would **"Race to the Altar"**
Only to become a guest on **"Cheaters"**
And find themselves saying **"I Want a Divorce"**
And the husbands were like:
"Well, **'Let's Make a Deal'** on the kids"

And as far as homosexuality,
You couldn't even think about being gay back then
Even though we didn't know that some of our priests
Apparently had a **"Queer Eye for the Straight Guy"** back then
But no **"Boy Meets Boy"** crap in my hood back then

Because folks were so ignorant
That when the Internet got popular they chose Yahoo!
Thinking hot-mail.com was a site for gay men

It's like in my 'hood there were 3 **"Fear Factors"**
Fear of homosexuals,
    Fear of commitment,
        And fear of the police

So no one in my hood watched **"Cops"**
Because if we wanted to get sneak peaks
At the lives of the police,
We could just walk outside and catch a live clip
Because they loved to shoot on location
Since they knew **"No Boundaries"**

So **"Murder in Small Town X"**
Was really murder in Boston, Massachusetts
Or anywhere America

But if you didn't get shot,
All you had to do
Was wait for clowns like Charles Stuart
To turn you into a **"Suspect"**
In a **"True Crime Story"**
And maybe if you were lucky,
You'd just get stripped butt naked in broad daylight,
Which was the **"Worst Case Scenario"**
After getting killed
Or losing someone dear to your life
Like when my man's 13-year-old cousin
Tiffany Moore
Got her brains blown off
Sitting on a mailbox one night

It was a **"Scary Life"**
Where you sometimes felt that you
Didn't have enough **"Adrenaline"**
To run this **"Amazing Race"**
Because I always felt
That it was **"The People Vs."** my hood
Since I grew up in a pseudo-**"Dog Eat Dog"** community,
Which was in need of an **"Extreme Makeover"**

47

That never happened

Because our governors were just politicians,
"Performing As" people who cared about our community
And even now they're trying to bring back **"The Chair"**
And **"The Chamber"** for the most malignant **"Offenders"**
Because there's no justice for the poor
In this system of **"Crime & Punishment"**

However, if you were a good **"Runner"**
Or if scouts knew **"Who's Got Game"**
Then you might have been able to leave your 'hood
And live that **"American High,"** **"Surreal Life"**
Where you were so **"Lost in the USA"**
That you forgot that you went
From **"Danger Island"** to **"Fantasy Island"**
Until **"Temptation Island"**
Brought you back down to earth
And you ended up working in **"The Restaurant"**
Right back on **"Danger Island"**

So take this **"Profile from the Frontlines"**
And don't be surprised
When you hear me talk about
How I sometimes find myself running from reality

Because sometimes I feel like I got lucky
Since in my **"Family"** there was no **"Faking It"**
Living with 8 other kids **"Under One Roof,"**
Often with too many **"Houseguests"**
"Crashing" with us in our **"Love shack"**
Where everything I owned was **"Public Property"**

But my mother,
She made us feel like we were all **"Celebrities"**
And let's just say my father,
He would give us **"Thirty Seconds of Fame"**
If anyone **"Wanted"** to act funny
And be the **"Last Comic Standing"**

I wish you could **"Meet My Folks"** and visit my 'hood
Because I was able to find love for my 'hood
And even find love in my 'hood

And become a **"Newlywed"**

So in reminiscing about my life,
I just had to put the pen to paper
So when y'all hear me recount these capers,
Ain't no need to turn on your TV
Whenever you wanna get a glimpse of a reality show
Just turn off your television and watch me
Or any kid living in the 'hood in this new century

Because our lives are reality shows
And so we're all filing a lower-class action lawsuit
To sue the creators of **"Survivor"**
For copyright infringement

The Inevitable Suicide Of A Wannabe Intellectual Revolutionary

Living the life of a lonely black man
Feels like being on a deathbed, on life's last strand
The days go by, and I just don't give a damn
I've fought to live for so long, now I'm on my last stand
You know loneliness is really the end of life, you see
Brothers can't survive without a woman, family and community
On the outside I look proud with my 'fro and its nappiness
But inside I'm crushed because I can't share my happiness
I walk with less bounce as I go here and there
Knowing that wherever I arrive, I'm always nowhere
I go where needed, and do what others need me to do
But they don't understand, I'm in desperate need too
But alas, I write, trying to solve my problems
Thinking this paper can help me resolve them
My dreams start to fade, aspirations start to crumble
My hopes for the future lay in a pile of rubble
I'm lonely Mother Earth!!!
Why was I given birth?
What is my purpose here?
What is life really worth?
There seems to only be room for brothers
Who are entertainers and sexual toys
But a brother tryin' to be intellectual?
Folks don't wanna hear that noise
Maybe if Malcolm and Martin played ball, they'd still be alive
Those were 2 of the loneliest brothers I've ever seen in my life
No one understood them, as much as they professed to
What I almost understand is that they were lonely too
They gave and gave, even when times got tough
Then this country silenced them because it had heard enough
These bold brothers knew their fate and took it strong
They knew fighting for liberty wouldn't permit them to live long
But you know what, they loved us, these strong, brave two
And they helped me realize that I love my people too
Thus, if fighting for my people is my destiny, I must go it alone
And realize I committed suicide a long time ago

Just Me

My name is Omékongo Luhaka wa Dibinga wa Yenga Kakesse
    But that's too much for many to try to pronounce
So they "affectionately" call me "O"
    And with that affection
Comes a certain type of subliminal interjection from their soul
    Because when they hear my poems,
The first thing that comes to their mind,
    Though they may not know is "Nah O!"
Don't talk about that political subliminal crap!

Don't talk about revolution & destitution in third world countries
    Don't talk about child pornography & secret photography
Of our black leaders in compromising positions
    Have you forgotten your position?
See you're a nigga,
    And nigga's don't 'posed to talk 'bout dose kinda things

Don't talk about Condoleezza,
    And killing a Congolese-a minute
In Western supported wars
    Just talk about the whores you see on BET
Who are probably only dancing to get through the university

Don't talk about feeling *insecure* in your home
    Because of homeland security
And how hearing this verse or version
    Will make a virgin to revolution scared to lose his virginity

Don't talk about West Indians trying to grow bananas
    And getting screwed
And don't talk about African presidents being used
    By foreign powers
And while you're at it,
    Don't talk about Rwanda and Samantha Powers
Or even Lumumba with Eisenhower
    Nah "O," have you forgotten that you's a Nigga
And Niggas don't 'posed to talk 'bout dat stuff?

Don't talk about perverted priests
    Who come to church to come in church
In the annals of their pure, pious pupils still being abused

51

And don't even talk about the Moulin or Khmer Rouge

Don't talk about child labor exploitation
    And Hollywood's on-going fascination
With stereotypical Asians
    And don't you dare talk about CIA covert assassinations
If you know what's good for you
    Nigga have you forgotten that you's a Nigga
And Niggas don't 'posed to talk 'bout dat stuff?

Don't talk about weapons of mass destruction in Iraq
    Or even about weapons of Mass-achusetts destruction
Like MCAS standardized testing
    When our schools don't have equal resources
Don't talk about
    Miseducation, miscegenation and misrepresentation
In the House and Senate
    Talk about football, basketball,
Or niggas and spics winnin' the pennant
    'Cause us niggas sure can run
And we don't get tired in the sun!

Don't talk about children dying in Chechnya
    Don't talk about those special-ed kids
Who really just have a slight case of dyslexia

Don't talk about police brutality
    And Americans superior-to-the-world mentality
Don't talk about cowboys, Indians
    ...and smallpox
And don't start talking about conspiracies
    Like the FBI killing Biggie & Tupac
Don't talk about myopic miscreants murdering homosexuals
    And don't talk about for whom the bell of revolution tolls

Talk about hip-hop and high-tops
    Talk about those black bitches,
Other ignorant niggas
    And those so-called wiggas, spiggas, and chiggas

Don't talk about deaths at the Belgian Battle of the Bulge
    Or even America's battle of the bulge with our diets
Don't talk about the President and the FBI
    Using F-B-I-s to get me to believe in *his* God

Don't talk about the CIA investigating MLK
    Don't talk about Cointelpro
'Cause we'll go-and-tell-pro black folks not to support you

And with all that Africa crap?
    Don't talk about FGM and HIV
And surely don't talk about the IMF and WB
    Strapping black economies
Don't talk about WMD like the WB, ABC and NBC
    Distortin' reali-TV for our children
Just talk about SUVs on BET
    And how we'll only become men,
Once we've been in prison
    Have you forgotten your position "O?"
You's a nigga and "niggas is a beautiful thing 'O!'"

Nah yo,
    See I've never been bamboozled into believing that myth
I was taught that a brother can read The Economist,
    The Source, and African Civilizations Lost
And still be considered a black man
    And why do I talk about places like Palestine and Um-Kasr?
Um, 'cause-r humanity is dying there with innocent people

So while you rant about the coming moment of truth,
    I'm more concerned with the truth of the moment
For while you demonstrate to the world your love of power,
    I'm gonna slay you with the power of love
And you keep trying to convince me that I'm a nigga
    Because it's gotta burn you,
You know, the fact that I'm writing this in a language
    That I wasn't supposed to learn too?

But let me remind you that my name is
    Omékongo Luhaka wa Dibinga wa Yenga Kakesse
So it's in my blood line to fight back
    Against any person or society that tries to test me

Because niggas is a beautiful thing
    In a world bent on domineering and mind control
But I believe there's still a place in this world
    For a righteous bro' with a righteous flow
So y'all can call me "O,"
    As long you know…

Oz, Can You Save Me?

I traveled the yellow brick road
On a quest for fool's gold
History untold, ancestors sold
In the name of you know who
Said my Voodoo was doodoo
And that it was libel to deface *their* bible

So I walked down this road
Into churches and schools
With pictures of my ancestors in chains
A whole continent in flames
So now I'm ashamed to call myself African
But I never quite felt like an American
So WHO am I?

Oz can you save me?
I'm more incomplete than Yurugu
A history stolen
My eyes swollen with knots from twin blows
Called Western religion and education
A misrepresentation of civilization
Heading towards cremation

But I must belong in this nation, the devil told me himself
He said I needed his wealth to complete me
And that loving my people will only retreat me
To the deeper depths of my African savagery
While he dastardly rapes my women and robs my continent
Not with colonialism but with investment

So I wanna be an American
Though his yellow brick road
Has led me to the highest levels of
Cancer, AIDS, high blood pressure, sickle cell, asthma
You name it,
I claim it

I gave my health to him
But worst of all,
When I look back in time

I gave him the most important thing I ever had
Peace of mind
And for that I have no one to blame but myself
Thus,
I must realize that Oz can't save me
I can only save myself

Runnin' From Reality

I'm runnin'
I'm runnin' from life
Because I'm afraid to live it
The fear of life has got me
Looking over my left shoulder
While with my right hand
I'm holding my wife's hand tight
Because I don't want her to trip
And fall into the reality of reality

And so I'm runnin'
And while I'm runnin'
I'm praying for all humanity
Before I lose my sanity
Because what's chasing me
Is a failed society

It's a society sweltering
With the heat of ignorance
Yet lacking emotion
Because most of our leaders
Were born during the Cold War
And my originality is sticking out
Like a cold sore
So I had to place myself like Marley into exile
Because I'm gonna meet Malcolm & Martin
Before I let this Matrix "Smith" me

And so I'm runnin'
I'm runnin' because I had the foresight,
To let my hindsight,
Influence my insight,
To improve my eyesight,
And that's why I have to write this

And don't be mad at me
Because that phalanx on my heels
Is penning this poem
And I tried to open people's pensive processes
But too many of them were trained

To only focus on historical fallacies
Which even had me
Screwed orally with rhetorical oratories

Until I realized that we're all living
In a state of denial
Because our governments preach peace
But their policies prove
They run states of denial
And as I dash I start daydreaming
Of dancing at the base of the Nile
Where I only needed to
Hope for a humble harvest
Instead of inconceivabilities
Like an international armistice
Of weapons in the hands of child soldiers

...And back in those ancient days,
Where we drew ankhs in the sand and...
!!!BLAM!!!

I'm clapped back into reality
Because society is now shooting at me
So I'm runnin' faster
With my wife now on my shoulder
And my future in my holster
But I can't shoot back at the beast
Because I don't have enough bullets

But BLAM!
Aargh!

BLAM!

Aargh!
BLAM!
Ah,
Damn!
Society's at it again!

And so with a couple of "civilization" shots
In my side,
I hide behind righteous rocks

To block the onslaught
Of society's gloc shots

So to flush me out from hiding,
High society's hurling
Javelins of injustice at me
Trying to pierce at the
Heart of my principles

And dodging bullets of indoctrination
While jumping over javelins of injustice
At the same time
Well,
That's like being a U.S. soldier overseas
You're caught between I-raq and a hard place
But the only coalition-of-the-willing I need
Is my wife

And so we run to the side of the right
And hide behind a
Marcus Garvey-sized maplewood
To let my afrocentricity
Hold down the fort

Because before this monster
Causes my pride to bleed,
Me and my wife are gonna conceive
Because I believe that I need to leave
A daughter behind
To slay this satanic society

And before I go back on the run,
I think about having a son
But the way that society nearly
Stripped me of my masculinity,
Making me think it was my destiny
To be complacent
Yet surrounded by drama
Having me decide whether
I wanna marry...or mari-juana
Making me think it was hip to hate me
As long as I loved He
And telling me that my life was a myth

And so I had to live *His* reality?

I now know that what the
World behind me needs
Is more feminine energy

But that relentless monstrosity,
He caught up with me
With a shank-full-of-sins
And he's stabbing me

So I've fallen and though he's
Standing over me
I still overstand
Because as I lay in the sands,
My wife and daughter
Hopped on Harriet Tubman's train
Because my seed, she's gotta train,
Since only a child's innocence
Can free this world from itself

But as for me,
I ran out of time
Runnin' from a society that couldn't realize
That though it was dying to live,
It was really living to die

But I fought the good fight
And like Morpheus I freed many minds
And so I went to meet my ancestors
With a smile on my face
Because I died a free mind
And didn't let society's
Dictates determine my fate
But how will you retaliate?

The African, The American

Some people desire to inquire
What my name means because it sounds so "powerful:"
"OMéKONGO"
Like I need to play some drums when I say it

Others ask if it's my "birth name"
As if it's any of their business
But short of the intrinsic inclination to input inhabitants in
Pre-determined non-pensive packages
Few people ask me what it's actually like
To be an American in Africa,
And an African in America

'Cause for real,
I feel like I need to relocate
To the center of the Atlantic Ocean
Because I am truly caught in the middle

The African, the American...
I'm remixing Angie Palmer's words
From "I've been rich and I've been poor"
To "I've been dissed and I've been torn"
Because I've been torn between being
Called the American nigga and the African bushboogie

I'm torn between having to speak "African"
To prove I'm African in America
And speaking French
To prove that I'm African
In francophone African countries
What???!!!

I'm torn between the gangs
And the "tribes" both practicing ethnic cleansing
I'm torn between seeing one set
Of my belabored brothers die for hot diamonds
And my other beleaguered brothers
Living to be iced out
But it still doesn't even out

I'm torn between
Trafficked African sex slaves having hymens torn
And American child porn
I'm torn between
Dealing with the child soldier
And the child gang-banger on the corner

I'm torn between
Dealing with African military leaders
Showing our kids they don't need school to rule
And rap artists telling our kids
They don't need school to be rich or cool

I'm torn between
Corporations using both
My communities as a toxic ditch
I'm torn between "I'm Mobutu Sese Seko"
And "I'm Rick James, *Bitch!*"

And I don't know
Whether to laugh or cry sis'
Because as proud as I am
To be who I am,
I sometimes feel like
I have an identity cri-sis

Now I know why
I'm so fond of "Transformers" cartoons
'Cause the way folks want me
To change up,
I might as well change my name
From Omékongo to "Optimus Dibinga"
Until people realize that
In getting past my name and frame,
There's "more than meets the eye"

But whether I be the American countryman
Or the transcontinental African
I know that both identities
End in "I-Can"

So I know I can be, be me,
Let my words do the talking,

And my actions do the walking

Because I will never fit into your box
Whether I got a fade or some locks
So when you're trying to figure out who I am,
And which stereotypical categories I cover,
I'll be covered in content
If you just called me, "That brother"

WATERING THE SEEDS OF GROWTH

Black Woman, I'm Sorry

Black Woman, I'm sorry,
For all the neglect
Over five hundred years here,
And still no respect
I really hope my apologies are accepted,
For not living up to all you've expected

But there's a force moving against us
It's like a brick wall
It's there to oppress us
And make sure we fall

We're set up to fail
Because they've set up the system
Though we're no longer for sale
A price is still given

They try to make us like them
To tear us apart
But so much unlike them
Our family's our heart

They've given us drugs
And TV aside
To teach us their methods
...A slow genocide

They make themselves look superior
To make us lose hope
We're made to look inferior
And take it as a joke

Black Woman, I've tried!
But the struggle is so hard
But with us side by side
It's worth the reward

So again we're learning
To support one another
To realize the strengths

Of you Sister and Mother

So please forgive us
We're steadily prying
I'll make sure we get there
Or Sister, die trying

Appreciation

I love you
Because you love me
You helped me find myself, you helped me realize who I am
You did everything in your power to make me be a real man

Once I realized that you were mine and I was yours
I knew our love combined could knock down any doors
You were there for me when no one else would be
And you have been for me what no one else could be

When the chips were down, you picked me up
And sacrificed and sacrificed so that I would never give up
Now many of you may think
I'm speaking of a wife, a girlfriend, or another lover
I'm telling you now to save the drama
Because I'm not talking about anyone else but my Momma

You see Momma, you saved me in this world of the unsaved
You taught me how to be proud and when to have shame
The love that comes from you emanates like sunlight
And since I've been loving you for 28 years
It's so much easier to love the other queen in my life

I can love my woman because she's a reflection of you
So I know that if I call her a "bitch," I'm calling you one too

You taught me to be proud of my blackness
And my masculinity
But you also said that since every man
Has an ounce of femininity
My black womanhood should come from the blood of Nefertiti

So for putting me on this earth
And making me feel worth
I owe you all that I have to give
And I will continue giving back to you as long as I live

Kendra

Baby,
You are the sun to my sky
Where I fly radiant red ribbons for our love
That leap over longevity
Like ebony angels over stagnant clouds
You are the spinal chord that's always got my back
When it's time to move mountains
And for those of you all who don't understand our love
Let me just tell you that when I'm away from her
All I do is have filling flashbacks of beautiful yesterdays
Of looking into the soul of this woman
And I just have to leave my surroundings and meander
Thinking about how me-and-her
Would spend the entire day
Shouting sweet somethings into each other's ear
In order to let the world know that our love flows eternally
Like the winding waterfalls
That so many seeking love end up chasing
While ignoring the running rivers and lamenting lonely lakes
That they're used to right next door
Well,
I realized at a young age
That in the abundance of water the fool is thirsty
So I jumped head first into the sea of your loving eternity
And now I just yearn to see your seductive smile
Bright up my life like shining, simmering sunrises
On melancholy, moonlit faces
Baby,
I would fly first-class across the world
Just to kiss you goodnight
So that I could be the last image you see
As you rest for the twilight
But it's partially in a non-altruistic aspiration
That you will dream of me in your dreams
As you sleep safely in the bed of fidelity
And though we're not at the level of mother and fatherhood
Waking up to your chiseled life sculpture
Makes my day pregnant with possibilities
Because I know I can get through the most dreadful days
As long as I can come home and be given rebirth

By the sweet sounds of your homilies
Honestly baby,
I was told that I was too young to marry
But that advice only came from part-time lovers
And since part-time lovers are part-time suckers
I vowed to give you all my love but not just half the time
'Cause baby, I'm not a Christian but lying safe in your arms,
I'm born again
I'm not a Buddhist but being with you,
I've attained a sense of private enlightenment
I'm not a Muslim but I attain a little sense of personal paradise
When I think of our affection
And so I never think twice about marrying my first and only love
And though times may get tough,
I bless Luther everyday for reminding me
That I'd damn sure rather have bad times with you
Than good times with someone else
So just know that as I look back and forth at the years of my life
I'll have nothing but purely positive thoughts
Of the years with my wife
Kendra,
You are my shining star and my African angel
So there's not a chance in hell of you losing my love
And even when I breathe my last breath and take my last step
Know that I will fly on cloud 9
Because you've brought my spirits so high
But until that day,
I'll continue to honor you
Because you complete me like a patient Yurugu
And so I write down these words
So that you and the world know
That my love for you is so real that it's surreal
Because you're like a fantasy making my mind run wild
Like leaves of love falling from the limbs of my poetree
And it's impossible to imagine
That these words couldn't have been conceived
If God didn't give birth to you,
Thus giving birth to trust
That gave birth to us
So let us walk in ecstasy down the aisle of devotion
As willing prisoners of each other's love
As our ancestors and God look proudly
In making two true soul mates merge into one

A Tribute To Black Women

Black Woman, you have always been there, leading the way
Without you I would not stand here, as I stand today
I don't know how you do it, how you keep on going
When away from you so many of my brothers are roaming

You've been raped, ravaged, had your name defaced
Yet still you've found time to be the backbone of our race
The backbone of our race, our heart, and our foundation
Even when we were stolen and forced to build their nation

When they took away our Ankh and gave us their cross
You kept your faith in God...a faith that I lost
I put my faith in my master, I wanted him to receive me,
But once he became my office boss, he no longer needs me

I thought I was alone, with no one to accept me
I turned to you and you were mad, but you didn't reject me
You never gave up on me, your love was so absolute
Even when I was angry and took it all out on you

I realize that I hated myself and that I did not hate you
I just did not know how to appreciate you

But my faith is back Black Woman! I have seen the light!
I realize I need you now, and not women who ain't right!
You see many are just curious and only lead us to their beds
But you're so divine you greet us with open arms, not open legs

You are on such another level, so surreal, so sublime
The only intercourse I want is intercourse with your mind
Just to hear your voice my body is yearnin'
'Cause I can make love to your soul, keeping my body a virgin

You are my future Black Woman, I know this once more
And with us side by side, better times are in store

I asked God what I needed to put me on track
God sent you through the door and I've never looked back
Brighter days are ahead, yes this I foresee
So to pay you this tribute, is an honor for me

Parler*

What does life revolve around?
You? Me? Eternity?
Could it be that it revolves around us?
Or do WE revolve around LIFE?

A husband, a wife,
Strife and chaos,
Lost love or maybe it never was
How could our love launch into decay?
Is it because we no longer parler?

I remember the day
When you began to serenade me
Outside my window
As I lifted my head from the pillow
I passionately let your mellifluous melodies sing a song
To my wintry and withered yet wanting soul

Was it you that I wanted
Your love that I saw?
That I knew would make me holy
In this world of flawed gods?

You crawled into my window
While everyone dreamt
Were THEY too dreaming of a love
That would be heaven sent?

Were they dreaming of an angel
Pursuing them through streets so methodically
Who would crawl through their windows
As the wind blows ever so melodically?

I meticulously mapped out our life together
But now our dreams have begun to wither away
Simply because we no longer parler

*Parler (pronounced "parlay") – "To speak" or "To talk" in
French

70

Dreaming Of Being Awake

Beautiful,
Lovely,
Black woman sleeping

Peaceful,
At Home,
Not a care in the world

Mother of the universe,
Sister of mine
So, so gorgeous,
And so, so divine

Dreaming of past, present, and future black greatness
Loving her people,
Yearning for unity

But alas,
She's a realist
And knows umoja* takes time

Thus, this queen,
So gentle and kind,
Knows she will wake up sad
In a world of racists, sexists, sellouts, and tokens
And so she sleeps with one eye open

*Umoja – "Unity" in Kiswahili

71

FALLEN BRANCHES

Losing Hip-Hop

Maybe my vision's a bit hazy
Or just call me plain crazy
But our brothers and sisters in the hip-hop business,
Never cease to amaze me

Remember you used to say:
"Hip-hop haters don't understand me"
Now you make a little bit of money
And hip-hop is for everybody?
Not realizin' you're a nobody
In your own profession

Haven't learned the lesson
Of cherishin' your black dollar
Buyin' Avarex, Versace, it got me yellin' damn,
Makes me wanna "Holla, Holla"
'Cause now you can't live without the "Prada, Prada"

You brag about
Goin' from havin' nothin'
To havin' somethin'
But now you're about nothin'

Went from singin' "I need love"
    To "I need an around the way girl,"
        To "I need a Gangsta Bitch,"
            To "I need a ride or die bitch"
From "I Need Love" to "A Ride or Die Bitch?"

Can't you see we're regressin'
While you're dressin' in Italian made clothes,
Rentin' Rolls for your videos,
Sportin' Rolexes,
And severin' any nexus to black pride

Singin' about Spanish Fly and half-black Filipinos
You wannabe gambinos!
Have you forgotten that
BLACK *IS* BEAUTIFUL
And that's where it's at?

Let's bring it back
'Cause you ain't makin' love
To your people no more

Whites buy 70% of your music
Until they find their own rappers
Someone really needs to slap ya!

Let's bring it back to the days
Of real out-the-back-of-the-trunk hip-hop
Back to the days
Of Public Enemy and Afrika Bambaataa
No more Prada
Let's rock the FUBU
And sing about Black Madonnas

You're too busy rappin'
In London and Amsterdam
That you don't see that
There are millions of Africans
Who'll do whatever they can
To see their descendants come home
And rock their stadiums and domes?

But alas, our people,
No longer slaves to pickin' cotton
Are slaves to rotten rustic lyrics
That espouse buying everything that's white
And killing our brothers
In the middle of the night or broad daylight
*   *   *   *   *   *   *   *   *
Maybe my vision's a bit hazy
Or just call me plain crazy
But our brothers and sisters in the hip-hop business
Never cease to amaze me

In 10 years,
Hip-hop music,
We WILL lose it,
If we haven't already
It'll be called "white music"
Like our children now call Jazz and Blues

It's good to no longer
Have hand-me-down clothes
And an empty stomach
But now you have an empty mind
And we're losing time

Each dollar saved on a hand-me-down
Was one less dollar spent outside our community
Now you can't wait
To buy from companies with "No Urban Dictates"

There are 6 million ways to be raped
And you're choosin' them all
And since you're gonna come crawlin' back to us
WHEN you fall

Let's get it together NOW
Hip-hop man & woman
Let's take it back to OUR streets
Where it all began

Losing Hip-Hop (The Remix)

This is a call
To all who claim the game
And embarrass our people
With lewd acts without shame
Because you never have to accept blame
For the state of our youth

Walkin' proud in your Hilfiger suits
And rappin' in rented cars
Makin' our children think you're big ballers
Packin' mad loot
But you're really only in pursuit
Of the booty

So you feel it's your duty
To lie to our soldiers
About your murder and STD immunity
While record executives
Let you spit your ignorance with impunity
Because they don't wanna see black unity

Since they take 17, 18, and 19-year old Nubians
Who think they're niggas
And promise them six figures
So these kids who don't even know
How to balance checks
Now perform with no checks and balances
Only thinking with their phalluses
Not realizing that malice is
Guiding their thoughts

We now have brothers who don't know their history
So they find strength in their hormones
And take pride in the ability to make a whore-moan
All while packing more chrome
All in the name of "Keepin' it real"

Not real-izing that hip-hop culture
Is really determined by CEO vultures
Hovering over ghetto projects

Waiting to pluck at the empty pockets
Of another lost mind
And promise to turn them
Into ghetto prophets
But makin' profits for record execs
Seems to be the only prophecy that comes true
So what can we do rap man?

Well we can start by following
Taalib Kweli's "Hip-Hop Manifesto"
And start kickin' relevant revelations
In our freestyles

And in the meanwhile
We can become hip-hop contributors
By learning to be black distributors
And earning more than $1.50 per CD sale
While posting $10,000 bail
For gun or crack possession
How many strung out,
Paroled,
Or murdered MCs do we have to see
Before we learn our lesson?

Do we have to wait for more of our sons
To lose their Shyne behind prison lines?
Or maybe wait to fall from the big time
By ending up like Biggie Smalls?
Or maybe have more Lost Boyz
Like Freaky Tah and Tupac?

See,
We're losing too many "Boyz in Da Hood"
Because we don't understand that
The "Scenario" has been remixed
And sent around the world
To make others think we don't love ourselves

So now we have to see that the Big L we lost
Pales in comparison
To the bigger "L" we're about to take
For our entire cultural continuum
Is now at stake, son

So if we could stop being "Fake Ones"
Then maybe we can resurrect this hip-hop nation

So to my rap man,
Nah, "I ain't mad at ya"
I'm just disappointed
Because our elders are out of touch with you
And so now Arista is your big sister
And you got big Warner Brothers
Teaching you how to be an ignorant black man

While Sony introduces your prepubescent mind
To his cousin, Virgin Records,
So you can get screwed for the first time
On contracts that you sign
With no consultation from independent lawyers

So nah rap man,
"I ain't mad at ya"
I'm just disappointed
Because too few have pointed out
The error of your ways

And so now these proud-to-be black niggas
Are approaching the "End of Days"
Where it's a matter of life or Def Jam
For consciously-deaf fans
Who don't wanna pump Mos Def
Because they lost their Common Sense
In their quest for green dead presidents
Instead of black ones
Because "It's bigger than hip-hop"
Right now as it always has been

You see hip-hop has been
In our soul throughout the ages
Even before Clive Davis
Decided to be a bad boy

Hip-hop had her history in Hausa-Fulani fables
Of call & response
And even in the Yoruba language
With Congolese nuances

Drumming its way
Through transatlantic slave voyages
And up through the plantation, Civil Rights,
Black Power, and Black Arts Movements

So once you realize
That hip-hop had no official start
Then record executives have no power
To bring it to an end

So to my rap man,
Stake your claim in this game
As its owner and king instead of its pawn
And to our elders,
Take our rappers by the hand
And walk them along through this concrete jungle
So they never have to wonder
Why hip-hop is going under

If we could come together
With the youth and the elder
We can truly take control
Of this hip-hop agenda
Because right now
It's "Self Destruction"
It's headed for self destruction

Act This Way

To our complacent
Black actors, athletes, and artists out there
I ask:
Where's the outrage?

Spending all of your time on stages
And forgetting what's going on
With our brothers and sisters behind cages
Like Maya Angelou's birds

It's absurd
'Cause it's like you ain't heard
That there are wars going on
In too many parts of the world

But you're only
Concerned with bling-blingin'
So you have no regard
For what you're singin'

Since you're only rappin'
About your bulletproof cars and vests
When your head's not mind-proofed yet

And them some of y'all
Drop these snippets of consciousness
Acting like you really love our sisters
Telling them to "Keep ya head up"
But it's only because they're on your knees
And they're too low to reach your testes

Then you got these artists
Claiming that they're hardcore
Down to the meat on their bones
But offstage,
They're vegetarian revolutionaries
Because there's no meat behind their words

And this is also absurd
Because you got these

Black actors and actresses,
Performing acrobatics on mattresses,
For academy awards
Telling our young queens
They can make it if they act like whores
Because deplorable images of women
Is what sells

And what the hell is up
With these brothers trying to be action heroes
When in reality
They're just Rambo Sambos
But since they're also
Playing revolutionaries sometimes,
They're more like Sambo Rambos

So "Hambo, Hambo, have you heard?"
I'm just trying to figure out
How to kill 3 mockingbirds with one poem
So leave me alone as I blast these rappers
With their chrome & iced-out Jesus pieces
While I'm seeing these so-called "conscious" artists
Sporting platinum star & crescents

While these actors play historical figures like Robeson
Who were about real revolution
And not ego-trippin'
But when it's time to look for y'all
At the real-life rallies
"Ain't no one here but us chickens!"

Or better than chickens
You're more like popcorn kernels
You're brown on the TV
But when the microwave heat of reality is put on
You pop white!

What the hell are you working for?
From Steppin' Fetchit to Steve Urkel
I'm sick of the cowardice and buffoonery
It's like all of your affluen-za
Has given you influenza
Because you've become cold to our causes

Since you're more concerned
With audience applauses

And I'm just mad
Because I can't get you in real life
To act like an activist
Because society's got you squeezed
Like a fresh glass of O.J.—Simpson
With poor blacks rallying
Because he was acquitted
And not giving a damn
That his politics never fitted our community
…Like a glove

While on dub,
Our musicians are "Holdin' it down"
From east coast to west coast to slave coast
With their platinum shackles
And football players only concerned
With making tackles
While I can't even get a quarter-back
On some reparations thrown my way

And in basketball,
Our kids don't give a damn
About the people of Iraq or Hebron's pain
Because they're too busy
Trying to be the next Lebron James

So to those celebrities who this applies to
Stop letting your status
Draw you from reality
And stop driving me to insanity
With all your profanity

You're getting million dollar signing bonuses
And you still ain't sayin' nothin'
While too many of us are content to sit calm
Watching sitcoms
And listening to whack songs
That we don't even care for what's on
As long as it has a nice beat

So we don't even realize
That our mind's being lulled to sleep
While white folks make TV shows
With child geniuses like "Doogie Howsa"
We're still "Bringin' Down Da House"
With movies like "Soul Plane"
And all that other "Yowsa, yowsa, yowsa"

So y'all just gotta forgive me
If I'm out of place
I'm just tired of seeing fake gangsters,
Inactive athletes,
And black folks
In black face

I want to see "our" celebrities respect our history
And learn to be more humble
Because they're single-handedly reversing
500 years worth of the struggle

True Poets (Or Lack Thereof)

I'm tired of watching spoken word poetry
Bring out the worst in us
It's as if mentally and spiritually
We're still riding in the back of the bus

I'm sick of poets performing perverted pathetic poetry
On podiums from Pasadena to Paris to Pretoria
And I'm sick of other poets pretending to be pious
And passing judgment on aggravated audience members
That these poets have never seen in their lives

I'm sick of poets coming up to curse the mic
With hopeless stories of insignificant others
And hypocritical lovers
With no explanation or evidence
Of having healed from their happenstance

I'm sick and tired of tired and sick poets,
Performing pieces that sound like thi-i-i-s
Copying Medina and the Last Poe-e-ets
And showing no originalit-e-e-e
And I'm not Jay-Z-e-e-e
But I thank God for grantin' me-e-e-e
This moment of clarite-e-e-e

Because I'm tired of poets talking loud but sayin' nothin'
And trying to cover up for their shallow words
By doing back-flips and Ma-trix
With little-to-no poetic sub-stance

Because I see right through their inept attempt
To focus on the performance
And NOT the poetry
Since I know it's not how you say it
But what you say

I'm sick of poets who haven't mastered the art
Of listening to their poetic peers
Only thinking their flows
Merit the ears of the crowd

And while I'm on this tangent,
Let me just say that I'm really tired and perplexed
By poets who come to the mic
Intent on dissin' each other

Because I can go to a dozen dialectically dirty open mics
And hear a dozen dirty poets
Still playing the dirty dozens
As if they were back on the plantation
And I can't help but wonder
What their poems would sound like
Before the Emancipation Proclamation

These self-proclaimed "field niggas"
Would probably be entertaining runaway slaves
In secret caves
With poems entitled
"On the Block" or "Let's Make a Deal"
With their partner in the background
Singing "Whip Appeal"

And folks would only snap
Not to substitute for a clap
But when the whip hit their backs
Or their baby's face

But even back then,
I'd be coming in Nat-Turner style
With poems inspiring insurrection
And these poems would be entitled
"Off the Chain" or "Off the Hook"
And I would try to make these poems
Sound so off the chain and off the hook
That all slaves who heard the words
Would want to get off the chain and off the hook

And this is what I ask from our poets!
Can we write words
That will incite us to uplift ourselves,
Or am I asking for too much?
I want poets to speak about the seriousness
Of staying silent in a system of societal strife

I want poets who have suffered sexual assault
To serenade us with soliloquies
Of survival and hope
To make us all wanna "Take Back the Night" *and* the day

And I want black poets
To serve as America's conscience
To remind this nation
Of the dangers of discriminating against folks
Because they're gay
I want our poets to be the pure platform
For the people
But am I asking for too much?

I once looked into the eyes
Of a recently raped Congolese refugee
And I knew that she would kill any one of us
For an opportunity to experience
The American dream *and* the American nightmare

And I juxtapose that refugee
With her dreams deferred
With you non-poetic patrons
Finding yourselves seeking refuge in poetry venues
Because I know you'd kill
For the capability to communicate with crowds
Like a poet
But you can't

So you flock to open mic spots
With half a hope that someone
Will speak what's on your mind
Only to be sent home time after time
Disappointed in the lines or the rhymes
Of broken spoken words

Because I know that there's a sister out there
Who wants to hear a brother spit a love poem
Without mentioning sex
And I know there's a brother out there
Who wants to hear a sister tell him
He's God's answer to her distress

And someone out there is hoping to hear a homily
That will give him the strength he needs
To go home and tell his family he's harboring HIV
And I know there's a teacher out there
Who wants to be to told that she's not a terrorist
But rather an underpaid,
Unappreciated soldier,
Seeking to save the soul
Of our nation's future

But we as poets,
We give you the same
Depressing and downright despotic diatribes
Mouthing off about our penis and vaginal size
While falsifying facts about our sex lives
In irrelevant dialogues
Just trying to poetically screw you
With our dic-tation and vagina monologues

And I'm just tired of these
Wanna-be divas and demagogues
Souped up in celebrations of self
Like they're bigger than what they are
Forgetting that they're poets and not superstars

And it's quite scary
Because soon these poets
Will be rollin' up to open mic bars
In fur coats, Bentley cars, and Jaguars
While the real representers of the word,
We'll be called "alternative" and "neo-soul" poets
Like India Ar...

But even with a CEO-selected title for our genre
We'll still be trying to raise the bar
For folks living behind spiritual and physical bars
And we'll make it okay for poets
Who are afraid to be labeled "bougie"
Because they're studying for the bar
And we'll welcome those rappers
Who don't think they're poets
Because they only flow in 16 bars

So I'm gonna take this same poem to 16 bars
And ask the same question:
If some spoken word poe-tree with some substance
Drops in the middle of an open mic spot
Can it make a sound?
Can it still be profound?

Can a love poet influence an indecisive brother
To go home and propose?
Or make a sister believe
That she can make a man love her
Before she takes off her clothes?
We as poets need to rethink our flows

We're steppin' to the mic
Intent on tearin' each other apart
While our government leaves our children behind
Since we forgot it's all about the babies

But we're too busy tryin' to impress folks
Because we read books like the Kama Sutra
Instead of trying to start reformations
Like both Martin Luthers
We're going from "I Have a Dream"
To "I got some C.R.E.A.M."

And it's just sad because I've seen
Too many hubris-hampered ho-ets
Come and go in 3 minutes like one night stands
After raping, sodomizing, and verbally assaulting the mic stand
Leaving it feeling violated, alone,
And yearning for companionship from compassionate poets
But am I asking too much?

Then if I am then we're all damned
Because if *this* is the destiny of man
Then I'm gonna have to die tryin' to make a stand
For the true poets

IF SOME POETREE
FALLS IN THE MIDDLE
OF SOCIETY...

Signs Of The Time

We are living in a world faced with war
On multiple mental and physical levels
We still got black wars against the police,
Crack wars in the streets,
Unemployment at its peak,
Overcrowded prison cells
In present-day hells,
Wars with Jews against Muslims
Over whether a created state Is-rael,
Wars over Wesson with Saddam,
American politicians arguing
Over the difference between smart and dirty bombs,
Instead of smart children in dirty schools

I'm feeling like it's me against the world
And I'm starting to get IL
Without even thinking of Kim Jong
Though North Korea does have the world
Turning up on its axis right now

With these signs of the time in mind
I wake up everyday with one burning question
And it takes me no fewer
Than 24 agonizing hours to answer:

Am I gonna die today?

See, I don't even bother watching my back anymore
Because I might get killed from the side today
Or maybe they'll finally get me n-u-clear
With bombs dropping from the sky today

Or maybe some religious fanatic
Will blow my behind up in a train station
After deciding he wants to get closer
To paradise today

Hell,
I gotta worry if an insane and depressed pilot,
Whose wife just cheated on him

And ran away with the kids
Is gonna fly today
Right into the 13th story of my building
Where I just called my wife
To tell her I got a rise in pay

Or am I gonna get hit on some *Driving While Black*
While driving on I-95 today?
Or maybe some crooked cop's gonna decide
That some no-good-nigga's mom
Is gonna cry today?
All this while wondering whether Bush
Is gonna play chess with our lives today?

Why today?

Instead of getting caught up in all that today,
I think I'm just gonna lose myself in the movement
This moment, I own it
Because it might be time to go
It only takes one shot for cops to release my soul
'Cause our community's stalked by filthy 5-0

So I've decided that I'm gonna fight today
Because there's always
Just enough time left to be right today
My kids are expecting for me to take a stand
Against wars in Korea, Iraq, and Afghanistan today

So I gotta fight for this world to be safe for we
And this is personal
Because I don't want my child to see my face
Next to the definition of complacency

So I'm gonna fight this system
With all of my might today
Because it's true that tomorrow never dies
...But I might today

Living in a world where our young visionaries
Are becoming so hopeless
That they're losing their sight today
And so many perverted priests and pedophiles out there,

That I gotta worry about whether
My sons and daughters are gonna stay tight today

While Bush gives the rich tax cuts
And the poor ax cuts
On educational spending,
My students,
They're expecting for me to do what's right today

Looking down at the end of the tunnel,
I woke up seeing the light today
Because nations may blow up entire other nations
Out of spite today
And though I have my cell phone on,
I might not have enough time
To call my mom and say goodbye today

Y'all may say that I'm paranoid today,
But inhaling historical truths has got me high today
So now I'm looking for heroines and heroes
To help us stop our plight today

I'm even wondering if all this second-hand smoke
Finally gave me cancer today
So I dialed 9-1-1 for emergency assistance
But Bin Laden answered today

See,
I just walk around thinking that
Something's gonna get me
And I wonder why the hell you never ponder
If you're coming with me

So you have to forgive me for recounting
Some of the signs of the time
That we live in
Because since ignorance is bliss,
I know some of y'all forgot the hell we done been in

Got me wondering if God
Is really gonna be forgivin' for all of our sinnin'
Like killing in each other
In the name of religion

All I know is that I'm gonna keep on fighting
And never give in

So if I die before I lay my head to sleep today,
I just pray to God my soul to keep—today

Hell

It has been said that
We are living in the greatest nation on earth
It has even been said
That we are experiencing an economic prosperity
Never known to mankind

Most homes have TVs and PCs
And many believe they will get that
Pot of gold at the end of the American rainbow

But are we really living in the best of times
Or the worst of times?
Because through time it has become quite evident
That we have never lived in a paradise
Of heaven-sent proportions
For if you take portions of everyone's respective lives
To form one collective memory
You would soon see
That we are all living in hell

For what does economic affluence mean
To the man who lost his family
Because he fell in love
With Wall $treet?

What do millions of dollars in reparations mean
To that Holocaust survivor
Who would happily spend her last dime
To see her family just one last time?

What about that African-American soldier
Slain in World War II at the hands of a Nazi
But whose family will not-see his name
In any of the history books?

And where is heaven
For that slave descendant
Who has yet to see his first dime
After 350 years of unpaid labor?

What does the chance at a great education
Mean though to that Latino

Who voluntary loses his language, culture, and history
In a vain attempt at assimilation?

Or what about that Native American
Who, in his own nation
Is refused his piece of the American pie
Because he arrived at the table without his reservation?

And what about that Korean employee
Working at McD's
Who can't even be proud of a war
Her people could have won
Because she lost her unarmed son at No-gun-ri?

And what about brothers
Given the death penalty
After already being sentenced
To life in hell as black men in America?

Is there really heaven on earth
For that immigrant-hired-help
Putting in maximum effort
For less than minimum wage?
Or that college-bound brother
Whose blood was smothered
In a case of road rage?

How can you sit there happily in peace
While little babies are crying and dying
Trapped in the Middle-East meets West
In a clash of civilizations,
While certain developing nations face starvation
Where children walk around
With bloated stomachs and emaciated bodies
While we walk proudly with
Bloated pockets and emaciated minds

Wearing our $200 sweatsuits
From a sweatshop run in Thailand by Reebok
And being too busy
Watching DVDs on our laptops
That we can't hear the gats pop-poP-POP
That killed Amadou
Which, ironically stopped

Just before they reached 42
Which in the time of Horus or Heru
Meant divine judgment
You see it's coming!

So can you emerge from your matrix
Long enough to see
That there can be no rich without poor
And no peace without war?

That there is only a need
For ivy leagues
As long as community colleges
Strive to be respected by the mainstream?

That there can only be
Developing nations at the bottom,
As long as developed nations
Live lavishly at the top?
And that there would be
No billionaire record executives
Without negative lyrics in hip-hop?

The next time you look into the mirror
Stare deep into your eyes and realize
That the good life for you
Is nothing but someone else's hell
So it's really just a gigantic wishing well

So let those of us who have experienced success
Bless the world with our knowledge
And not live comfortably
On the edge of selfishness

For if you spend your entire life
Devoted to material wealth,
While drinking and smoking yourself
Into declining health

If you choose not to take the time
To serve those less fortunate than we
Then hell will be arriving at your door
Must faster than you can blink
And sooner than you think!

Proselytizing Penis

There was once an 11-year-old boy
Who believed in 3 things:
His mother, his grandmother, and God
Now his mother and grandmother he could see everyday
But he could not see God
And that is why he went to church
And it was at church that he met Father Pastor

Father Pastor told the boy
He could show him the way to God
All he had to do was meet him at his house
One day after church
And so the little boy went in search of God

The young boy was fascinated
By the way in which Father Pastor spoke the gospels
That he believed Father Pastor
Would actually show him the way

And so when Father Pastor said:
"Always be at church on Sunday,"
He obeyed

And when Father Pastor told him
To always listen to his Momma,
Who told him to always listen to his pastor,
He obeyed

And so when Father Pastor told him
To bend over and strip down butt-naked,
He obeyed

For 7 weeks, this young boy was reduced
To a walking rectum
By a sadistic, self-proclaimed, servant of the Lord
Who plastered him to the wall
As he sodomized any semblance
Of self-respect from his spine

This young boy
Already a gracious gift from God
Became a pastor's playmate in search of God

Believing this was the way to meet his creator

But,
After 7 weeks of unkept promises by this pornographic pastor,
After 7 weeks of a blood-soaked anus ,
That was always dry by the time the little boy got home,
The young boy grew suspicious of Pastor's proselytizing penis
Wondering why he always said "In God we trust"
When his eyes were only baptized with lust

          And so **1** day during his repeated rape
    The little boy had a "**2**nd" coming
       You see it was his **3**rd eye telling him he had
              Just **4** minutes to free himself-how? You see,
         He had **5** centuries of sodomized slavery survivors
Saying to listen to his **6**th sense and free himself
        From these **7** weeks of hell by having Father Pastor
     Sentenced to **8** years
        In a **9** x
          10-prison cell

And so on the 7th day,
Father Pastor was a-rrested
But who the hell will save the mind
Of this emotionally scarred boy
Who has yet to see God?

Always count on Grandma to make things right
You see his grandma told him that
As long as he strived to be God-like
He would see little bits and pieces of God
Everyday when he wakes up and looks in the mirror

And so this boy,
Forever scarred by a perverted pastor
Who promised him the Messiah
Knows that he will see God,
When God says it is time

And though he can no longer walk straight
Because of his ordeal
He knows that if he walks
In a straight path with God
His soul will forever be healed

98

The *Dietribe* *

Hi
How are you?
Ever get that "not-so-thin" feeling?
Ever wish that you could look down and see your toes
Without having to bend halfway over?
Ever wake up wondering
How you can turn that 2-liter into a 6-pack
Without doing a sit-up?

Well you're not alone,
See millions of Americans in this *Fast Food Nation*
Are just like you
But have no fear
Science is on your side
Because now you can lose all the weight you want
And you don't even have to exercise

To hell with running, walking, bike riding and eating right
Because nowadays
They got pills, potions and diet programs
To perfectly keep us all looking tight

Hell,
Why get up and do a sit-up
When you can get one of those "Ab-Aways"
And vibrate all day
Until those pounds just wither away?

Or you can just try diets
Like Jenny Craig, Atkins, Jack LaLane or any other kind
As long you can stay in that McDonald's line
And out of the gym

Science got your back man
So if you wanna lose that fat man
Don't lose hope,
Drink more Coke
Because you'll never have to jump rope again
You don't have to do pull-ups,
Jog, or get in the ring and bob & weave

Damn it,
Real soon you won't even have to breathe
Because they're concocting new formulas
To suck that fat right out of you in one swoop!
                                                    Whoooooooosh!
It's better than liposuction!
You can go from the Blob
To Tyra Banks or Wesley Snipes
Get that body looking tight
Without ever having to eat right

No more need for fruits, vitamins,
And vegetables for dinner
Because new technology
Will keep you looking thinner

And for you poets out there
Do you know how I stay slim?
I've created my own new formula called "Poetrim"
I recite 5 poems a day but at key hours
And the excess weight just comes right off

But only if the poems are 3 minutes, 10 seconds tops
Otherwise I'm wasting my time
While augmenting my waste-line
*   *   *   *   *   *   *   *   *
I know I may sound like I'm joking,
But I'm really hoping
That we'll take better steps to improve our well-being
Because we're seeing that Americans are becoming larger
As the search for quick fixes reaches new heights

Because we wanna be able to watch 8 hours of TV a day
And ruin our sight,
Play-Stations all night,
Poison ourselves with mad cows and Sprite,
And still ask "How can I lose this cellulite?"

Is this not ludicrous?
Haven't you simply realized that you are what you eat
Or you eat what you are?

Didn't that little yellow cartoon germ tell you that
"You are what you swallow"
So stop eating crap like there's no tomorrow?
Isn't it that simple?

I've had children in my literature class
Literally eating frosting for breakfast
While many misguided Muslim children
Break-fast at Burger King
So they never truly purify themselves

For we live in a society
Where little kids with asthma have strokes
Because McDonald's is the new home-cooked meal
For breakfast and lunch
With Kentucky Fake Chickens for dinner
And leftover Sara Lee Cheesecake for dessert

It hurts for me to have to say all this
But too many of us are losing our work-out-ethic
Spending more money
So we can move less and eat more
While many of the world's poor
Eat one meal a day

See, this is all unnerving
Because here we're not even serving
Our kids what they need
So on both sides of the world
Our children are malnourished
Since the fast food industry uses
Subliminal criminal messages
To attract our children to trash,

And then we wonder why they have
Increasing rates of heart disease and diabetes
While our kids are still in their teens
Since the federal government
Feeds them the same crap in our schools

Oh God I ask you how have we become such fools
Intent on poisoning ourselves by eating hamburgers

Composed of 30 different cows
And we can't even drink 8 glasses of water a day

And now obesity is supposed to be genetic?
How pathetic are we becoming
When we search for ways
To blame our forefathers and foremothers
Instead of eating less potato chips, ice cream,
And movie popcorn with extra butter

The Fast food industry makes billions of dollars annually
Simply because we've lowered our health standards
While increasing our intake of food flavored
With chemicals and animal waste
Because in the production process
Our food loses its original taste

But I'm probably wasting my time
Since many of you have already decided to die early
By the way that you dine
But before you leave here to go to IHOP
I hope that you take heed of these words

Because the world's richest nation
Has become the most obese
And won't live long enough
To enjoy the fruits of its labor
Because fruit is no longer part of the diet

But if you want to join me
In this battle to save our lives
You must understand the words of my dietribe,
Eat right and exercise,
And we can reclaim our physical well-being
One pound at a time

*Partially inspired by Eric Schlosser's Fast-Food Nation

My Inbox Is Boxing Me In

My inbox is boxing me in
The four corners of my computer screen
Have conspired with my keyboard
To coax me into a crusade of constant communication
Often with myself:

"Damn him for not writing me back"

"How can no one write me on my birthday?"

"Do I want to increase the size of my... wallet?"

"Do you REALLY think I want your stinkin' credit card?

Actually, I do, but that's not the point!

My inbox is boxing me in
I know the computer is saying "You've got mail"
But it might as well be saying "You've got hell"
Because once I log on
I have a devil of a time trying to logoff

As they say
"Idle hands do the devil's work"
Hell,
Sometimes even until my damn fingers hurt

I'm soiling my soul
By continuingly clicking the "refresh" icon
As if a new e-mail will purify my psyche
While drawing me to new advertisements by Nike

But wait!
        "You've got ma..hell!"
YES!
I knew someone cared!
Damn the fact that the newest e-mail
Is for an overdue credit card balance!
The fact that Visa believed
That I was important enough to write,

When NO ONE else wrote me in the past 3 minutes
...on my birthday,
Turns my hell to heaven
Until I click the refresh button again, of course

My inbox is boxing me in!
I've fallen victim to Satan's temptations
Risking consummation with computer viruses
After convincing myself that I really know "Melissa"
And cursing her for not writing me in so long

And as her birthday well-wishes
Corrupt my hard drive and soft feelings
Causing the files to erase
And my soul to become debased,
My fingers are left with no other recourse
But to write these words on paper

Paper?

If only people loved me,
And forced me to improve myself like my e-mail does,
I might have to kill someone

Tired Of Technology

Can you just follow me as I take you on this odyssey?
I'm tired of technology tapping me
On my shoulder
Everywhere I go like virtual Gestapo

You got cameras in dressing rooms,
And 3D cartoons that put Romper Room to shame
And then,
Like Mos Def said,
"I need ID to get ID"
Even though last time I checked
I still looked like me

You got felines that flush their crap
Down little cat toilets
And canines with collar-IDs
That holla whenever they get lost or detect fleas

But pardon me
As I get to the real bone I got
With this current technological progress
I'm talking about these cell phones

These cell phones are like cigarettes of the new millennium
Like cigarettes, they seem to come out of nowhere
When someone invades your air space
Not by smoking in your face but by yapping in your ear

And I fear like cigarettes
That excessive cell phone use
Can cause cancer
And it's no longer a rumor
Because research has shown that people got tumors
In the shapes of their cell phones
On the left side of their domes
Because that's the side
They always use to phone home

I know I use my cell phone too
But I got enough sense to know

That the person sitting next to me
Might not give a damn
To hear me telling my momma:

> "Hey Ma, I just got off of work at 2,
> And I'm at the train station about to get on the #2
> But oops! I gotta bend over and tie my shoe,
> Like you taught me too,
> And Momma—I LOVE YOU!"

I mean damn!
I just do unto others as I want done to me
Because I know I could frankly care less
If you just broke up with Jeff or Princess
   Or just lost a game of chess
         Or fake right and go left on the basketball court
Just turn off the damn phone
And tell them when you get home!

For goodness sake,
Just the other day,
I saw a baby in a stroller
With hydraulic wheels & a TV in his hood
ON HIS CELL PHONE
And he was just chillin', talkin' about:

> "Yeah, I'm on my way to the daycare
> So I'll holla when I get there"

And I'm thinking:

> If you're old enough to talk on momma's Motorola,
> Then what the hell you doin' in a strolla?

And that same night, I went to the club
And I was trying to exchange numbers with this sister
Thinking she would be impressed
By my nice PhD pen
But she was looking all unimpressed
And sweet and calm
As she pulled out her palm pilot
And I was like "Damn!"
As I promptly preceded to pretend

That I left my palm pilot at home
But it was already too late
Because I looked like a scrub at the club
All because of this damn technology

*   *   *   *   *   *   *   *   *

Seriously my people,
This will indeed be a mind-monopolized, Microsoft millennium
With Pentium-processed people polluting the air
With their stoic stares
But does anyone care to know that technology neither brings
Nor is the mark of civilization?

Can't you see that countries
That are becoming more technologically progressive,
Are becoming more violent?

Can't you see that we have
More access to telecommunications,
But less community?

Can't you see that we have
More access to knowledge,
But our children are becoming dumber and dumber?

I'm teaching children
Who cannot find the entire continent of Africa
On a world map
While one student told me that Massachusetts
Was the capital of Boston

While the only Austin he knew was Stunning Steve
Because he was on MTV
Which stands for Much-Too-Violent society
Where brothers shoot each other in the 'hood with bazookas
And paratroopas dropping from their ghetto bird nests
Invading where I rest with their shady arrest warrants

I wish I could just trade these times for simpler times
When I didn't have to dial an area code to call next door
And tel-a-marketer
To stop trying to sell me crap from their stores
Or even worry about everyone knowing
What I bought at the grocery store

And I'm tired of Big Brother
Hovering over me on highways and byways
Taking my license plate as I travel state-to-state
Don't you get irate when you contemplate this nonsense?

I would definitely trade these times for simpler times
If it means I could have a bit of my privacy
And you're all blind not to see
That the entire world is becoming computerized like Cybertron
But I'm gonna use this key to Vector Sigma
And bring it back to the natural

So you should be alarmed but stay strong
In realizing that fast cars, cell phones and skyscrapers
Are not the signs of physical, spiritual and mental health
They're just the signs of how a materially-driven
Egocentric people build monuments to themselves

And leave legacies by cursing buildings with their names
Instead of being remembered by non-financial deeds
That could teach our children that monetary success,
Without maintaining their basic humanity is not what they need

I wish I could just stab all of this unnecessary technology
And make it digitally bleed to death
Because no matter how many fast cars you drive
And how many millions you save
By the time you die
You can't take any of that to your grave
When it's time to see if God will save your soul

But if you're not feeling what I'm saying
You don't have to condemn and bother me
Just take this message from a brother
Who's just tired of technology

Asante Sana

As you sit down to enjoy your Thanksgiving dinner,
I just wanted to say thank you
I want to thank you for turning your back on all Native
Americans

I watch you brothers and sisters
At the Cleveland Indians games
Proudly wearing your Cleveland Indians hats
In support of Native American persecution

You have become a mascot wearing the hat of a mascot
Proudly wearing the Indian grin with your Sambo smiles
Even at the Blackhawk's game you got the same old excuse—
No excuse
When you're watching the toss of the pigskin
At your Redskins game
Your excuses are always lame

Did our ancestors persevere
So that you could have the right to not be called niggas
But to call homosexuals faggots
And ALL aboriginal ethnic groups Indians?

You can't think that since you got the right to vote
And a historically lop-sided education
That all other genocides can be excused

Don't get it twisted
Saying you're one-quarter Cherokee
Doesn't excuse the ignorance

I don't understand how you,
A people who have
Suffered under a savage system of slavery and suppression
For half a millennium
Could have forgotten the annihilation
Of those whose blood was laid before you
And lies inside of you

You think you've arrived
Though you are still despised by those you aspire to emulate
You dine on your swine at this time for family
While Native families fight extinction
Like the bald eagle or the conscious black man

But I'll be damned if I stand for this sham of a holiday
That should be a holy day for the original American

How can you proudly eat your peach cobbler
In honor of civilization robbers
Who spread the legs of natives apart
Like the wings of a vibrant dove
And repeatedly raped them of their culture?

Well,
If you want to sip from the wine of another's sorrow,
I'll leave you be
But just remember, when you sleep with suppressive snakes
The next Thanksgiving dinner may be in honor of you and me

Progress
(Or)
Excuse Me, Do You Have The Time?

I'm walking
    I look at a white man
He's scared of me

If I stand outside at 2 a.m.,
    With 5 or 6 of my friends,
I'm breaking *some* law

I'm walking
    My eyes fall upon a beautiful mansion
The only black people inside and out
    Are mowing the lawn,
        Or preparing dinner,
            Or rocking someone else's baby to sleep

I look at the paper
    An attack by Klansmen left 2 brothers dead
I look at the pictures in a well-known magazine
    And the blacks inside,
They all look like clowns or thieves
    America hates me

A white woman kills her babies,
    And the nation blames me
A white man kills his wife,
    And the nation is on a manhunt for me
Do they want to lynch me?

I want to tap that white woman on the shoulder
    And ask her for the time
But she might cry "Help! He's trying to rape me!"
    Now tell me,
Is this the 18th, 19th, 20th, or 21st century?

Privatizing Life

By the time you finish reading this,
17 children worldwide will have lost their lives
Because 8 children die a minute
In pursuit of potable water in order to survive
Partner that with the loss of husbands and wives
And you may end up cursing your eyes
Because you know these preventable mortalities will rise
Since water is now being privatized

Fed up with monopolies over diamonds,
Gold, coltan, and coal
Man is now on a mission
To monopolize Mother Nature's soul
No longer able to swim and drink
From our world's deltas and tributaries
Fees for life-giving water
Will have to be paid to evade the obituaries

Structural Adjustment Programs
Have become the equivalent of fasting
For our world's poorest governments
Must privatize water for loans everlasting
African Growth & Opportunity is being stunted
By acts most tyrannic
While corporations scramble for water rights
In a Berlin Conference-style panic

The rights of the human and earth
Are no longer relevant
For the right to profit
Now sets the precedent
Lower water standards and a depleted water supply
Are soon to follow
As Mother Earth becomes the liquid-deficient
Mars of tomorrow

From blood diamonds to "blood water,"
History is rearing its third eye
Forewarning us of the coming strife,
Which we can no longer deny
Civil wars will be waged

In the wanton pursuit of the world's water
Re-creating conflicts reminiscent
Of present-day patterns of slaughter

The developed world often acts
In the most undeveloped methods
By capitalizing on the lifeline
Of impoverished livelihoods
From protecting corporate interests
To interring corpses
The IFIs* have joined in the trademarking
Of our life-giving resources

But many of us will fight this battle
And that should now be apparent
For we won't allow the blue bloodline of Mother Earth
To become a patent
As man's oil of the new millennium
The poorest of the poor dangle their lives
Below profit's pendulum

Remaining inactive is an act in support of privatization
And the death of man
So the blood of the 17 children that just died
Also lies on your hands

*IFIs – International Financial Institutions

What Does Development Aid Really Mean?*

What does development aid really mean?
Does it mean managing money to mobilize against HIV
Or driving through southern Sudan in an SUV?

Does it mean the improvement of life,
Since many join the development enterprise
To improve their lifestyle?

Does it mean giving 1/10 of 1% of your GNP
And having 1/3 of that funnel its way to those in need,
Since most of the aid goes to pay aid agency staff salary?

What does it mean?

Development aid is well-intentioned
But in this new millennium
We have to learn our lesson

Because I'd rather have no aid than slow aid or low aid
If it means that development agencies will give funds
To governments for pipelines and pesticides
But indirectly support a genocide

Or have we forgotten the extreme case of Rwanda,
Where 80% of development aid
Went to the pre-genocide government
Even though all of the signs
Of the genocide were in place

But agencies for aid
Paid it no mind as long as that well-water became potable
     ...or that fertilizer ferry became floatable
          ... or that minimal rise in literacy became notable
Just noticeable enough to give
Uplifting quotable statistics on reportbacks to donors

Please!
Misguided, top-down development
Enforces the politics of exclusion
Because in collusion with repressive governments,

The poorest of the poor never receive assistance
In fields like subsistence farming

And it's quite alarming
Because aid agencies
Never realize their agency in societal conflicts
Because they claim to take an "apolitical" approach

But they fail to see how misdirected,
Top-down aid can encroach
On a politically fragmented society
And exacerbate it
By further disempowering the disempowered
Primarily by working with government-appointed elites

So we have to rethink development
Because many of us don't understand
What to "develop" meant in the first place

I'm even calling for a structural adjustment program
Of Structural Adjustment Programs
And other policies that claim or claimed
To assist developing homelands

Because development doesn't mean
That we can have true African Growth & Opportunity
When the resources we use
Don't come from our own community

Aid doesn't mean fancy dinners in classy hotels
With money given to decrease mortality rates
For newborn children

And if aid can't be given to a government
Without a care for ensuring the rights
Of every child, woman and man
Then I'll be damned before I say
That everything is "okay" with development aid

*   *   *   *   *   *   *   *   *

It's time to ensure that our dollars are being spent
On education and public health
As opposed to Safari vacations and private wealth

For foreign experts and host government hierarchies

And if we can have vouchers at home
Why not have developing country vouchers
So good governments can choose
The best development projects for their land
Instead of generic plans from those
Claiming to know what's best for the world's destitute?

Development aid can't be looked at as a
Wall Street business transaction
Where investors are only worried about the comeback

We need to come back and revise our strategy
Because we'll all be glad to see the day
When development aid is not *only* concerned
With promising statistics on cocoa revenues, crop distribution,
And more village midwives

Because few lives will be improved or saved
Unless the poorest of the poor
Truly receive the majority of the aid

So until the day when
Underdeveloped development dreams
Are redeveloped for developing countries
Development aid will never be what is seems

And if we continue to turn a blind eye
Or a deaf ear to this preventable predicament
Then the poorest of the world's poor will continue to ask:
"What does development aid really mean?"

Partially inspired by Dr. Peter Uvin's Aiding Violence

"A NATION WITHOUT KNOWLEDGE OF ITS HISTORY...

The Love That Hate Produced

This is a story about love
But it's not about that Valentine's Day love
Or that motherly love
It ain't even about that Philly brotherly love
This is a story about the love that hate produced

It's a story about Africa and all of her children
Still loving themselves
After centuries of systemic injustice
It's a story about tragic, transatlantic treason
And Berlin boundaries being drawn
Across ethnic lines with no rhyme or reason

It's a story about enslaved Africans beating the odds
And nations conquering other nations
And changing their monotheistic gods
By creating missionary positions,
To screw Africans in missionary positions,
In order to religiously rape them of their own religion

It's a story of Europeans using "civil lies"
To try to "civil-ize" the creators of civilization
And a story of Klan rallies and white families
Gathering on a sweltering Sunday afternoon
Around half-past five
For a friendly game of
"Blacks being burned alive" at the stake
And living for over 300 years as enemies of the state

It's a story about Langston Hughes
Through poetry shaping the Blues
And stereotypical images
Of black men on the news

It's a story about Jesse Owens
Humiliating Hitler
And then being humiliated upon his homecoming
Where he was still treated like a 2nd class citizen

It's a story about Kings
Losing their crowns on Tennessee balconies
And Malcolm's slaying
For pointing out white fallacies

It's a story about Joanne
Going from America's daughter
To persona-non-grata
Under the name of Assata

It's a story about Congolese genocide
In the name of coltan, diamonds and gold
And about southern Sudanese slaves
Still being sold in this new millennium

It's a story about Garrett Morgan
Creating the gas mask
That would save the lives of millions of firefighters
Who would then turn hoses on our people
Igniting an international fight for civil rights

This is about that production process!
Manufacturing love
In fascist factories
And capitalist corporations

It's a story about Queen Mothers giving Moore meaning
And life to the movement
And Muhammad's messages to the black man
And marches on Washington

It's a story about Reverend Bernice
Picking up her father's crown
And Malcolm's children preventing his legacy
From being bought and sold on the down-load

It's a story about Allah sending us honorable ministers
To expose sinister servants of Satan
And Final Calls giving us our marching orders
On how to rebuild the black nation

It's a story about Marian Anderson
Shining on the Washington Monument stairs
After years of contempt from her peers

It's a story about Tuskegee Airmen
Being humiliated and discriminated against
But never flying their planes into the World Trade Center
Because our people are too forgiving
In the face of ingrates
Who don't appreciate our good natured-ness

It's a story about Ali
Standing strong in protest of Vietnam
And Sam Cooke's swearing to the death
That a "Change Gon' Come"
As Major League Baseball welcomed Jackie Robinson
Though Fritz Pollard's family still looks for recognition
In the should-be-shamed NFL Hall of Fame

Nevertheless,
It's a story about Serena and Venus Williams
Picking up Althea Gibson's greatness and Arthur's ashes
And winning at Wimbledon
And Tiger's making all competition retreat into the Woods

It's about conscious brothers and sisters in professional sports
Who have taken it upon themselves
To take care of their 'hoods
And hip-hop artists protesting
To keep our education system from becoming no good

It's a story of brothers dying
On the front lines of Korea, Vietnam and Kuwait
So that the world could see
The first black Secretary of State

It's a story about the nation's defense
Being placed in the hands of a sister
And about Lauryn's climb up her Hill to humility

And a government trying in futility
To break our attempts at unity

It's a story of a people
Becoming black and proud
And not being afraid to say it loud

Can you hear it?
It's the sound of all the love and hugs
Being exchanged at the millions of marches
And our people committing themselves to health
And not the golden arches

It's a story about a people
Reclaiming its African identity
Like rollin' on from Roland to Askia
And international protests to try to free Mumia

This is a story about love
In the face of a system that hates us
But can't live without us
But most importantly
It's a story about God's chosen people
Rising up from the dust

This is a story,
About love

The Struggle

America,
Land of the free
Home of that brave slave
Who fought so that you could vote
Even though you don't

A land where you can fly high
Like a bird in the sky
Or be dragged like a Byrd
Through the streets of Jasper, Texas

A land where blacks run around
Like we don't know who we are
And have a record company
Make us superstars?

You see this is America
Where you can get paid to be ignorant
Get more props coming out of jail
Than tryin' to be diligent

Indigent is what we are,
Spiritually decadent
Blamin' ourselves for slavery
While the white man has yet to repent
Damn,
He must be heaven sent

We feel we have to go to school where he went,
Pay him rent,
Smile in his face and always act content,
Spend $700 billion a year building *his* encampment,
While spending on us just 7%?
Thinking if we go to a black school it'll be any different,
When in black & white schools they control the endowment?

How the hell can you rise,
When you keep looking at yourself
Through the shotguns he calls his eyes?
When you're afraid to speak proudly

Of your beautiful black skin
Because you have a fear of offending him!

You can never win
Until you wake up from within,
Learn who you are and experience jubilation
Like a nigga realizing he's an African!

You see, we have trouble uniting
Because we don't trust each other
Neither sister,
Nor brother

We are dying my black family
And I know you can't stand me
Because of what I'm saying
But we need to stop playing

Look at you!
Descendants of Almighty Africans
Trying to be Egocentric Europeans
And doing a horrible job at that!

Running around like chickens
With your heads cut off
While putting polluted, decomposed
KFC "chickens" in your bodies
Killing yourself both physically and spiritually

The time is late, the hour is now
We need to stand up black family
And be black and proud
And say it loud!

Because we're in America
But America ain't got to be in us
We need to rise up like the dust
In this sandstorm called white supremacy

Stand proud of your blackness
Because it's all you got
Stop prostitutin' our race
As if no one ever fought

So that you can be in America
And enjoy all you do
Use this system but don't let it use you

Let's get it together black man and woman
Let's support our own businesses
And own our own land
It's now or never
So if you don't start acting
Like you're proud to be black
Then give it back!
The lips, the hips, the naps, the sack
Just give it back!
And lie down and die
From that spiritual bullet in your back!

There Ain't No Struggle

How can you assassinate leaders in every country overseas,
But not find out who killed Jean Benet-Ramsey?

How could you assassinate Malcolm X
And then call him a civil rights champ?
Declare him a hero and put his face on a stamp?
It's because my people let you

We let you pump drugs in our 'hood
And then say we're no good
Man if I could kick you out of office I would
Oh shoot, I could...if I voted
But nah, I'd rather complain
'Cause ain't nothin' better than passin' blame

While you droppin' bombs
On people that look like me
I'm too busy sportin' Tommy and DKNY
Why?
Because I don't give a damn!
I blame you because I don't care
About my fellow black man

I don't care about nothin'
But nuttin' inside some hopeless whore
Since you hid my history
What makes me proud?
It's ridin' high
On a cloud of my own ego

It's the fact that my clothes
(Which you made)
Look better than yours

White man,
I'm your most powerful weapon
More lethal than nuclear missiles and crack cocaine
I'm an ignorant black man who loves passin' blame

Why act when I can react?

Be proactive?
That's whack
I'd rather lay my brother flat on his back

And since I don't respect or value my sisters,
I just keep makin' love to hoes
And havin' sex with queens
Knah' mean?
I can kill 2 birds with one loaded penis

And you know what?
There are millions of us
You can catch us at the back of the bus

Get involved in the struggle?
You buggin'!
That's crazier than naming tank tops
After abusive husbands

So go ahead and keep bombin'
While I'm robbin'
You kill the black folks over there
I'll take care of my people over here

Keep payin' me and I'll keep singin'
'Bout us bein' niggas and bitches
And not respectin' ourselves
You just concentrate on tryin' to make
Latinos and Asians into honorary whites
They'll do you right

I'll take care of my own
I'll destroy their minds
Just remember it's *your* fault not mine
You put that spiritual bullet in my spine

Rise Up Black Man

Rise up Black Man
Rise like the rush of a
Million men marching up mountains
Moving to obtain their mental manumission
Let African pride be your ammunition
And let's engage in sedition if we must
Because it's up to us to uplift our nation
From the dust of dreadful damnation

Rise up Black Man
Rise like a million men marching
Against the tide of societal injustice
Rise like a Nubian phoenix
Turning that flame that burns incessantly on your inside
Into a torch that you take to toss
On to the next generation
So that they can take that flame
And frame a resilient picture of our future

Rise up Black Man
Rise to the occasion
Show the world how black men
Are still in the households and not in jail
Still pursuing that education
And proudly paying tuition and not bail

And you,
You bold black men on lockdown
Must show the world that you got your head up
With your eyes on the prize
Because that prison cell you're in
Could just be a blessing in disguise

Even in the prisons
Where we live like slaves Black Man
You have the power
To break those chains or handcuffs
And collectively we'll call everyone's bluff

Because we got too many fakers out there

Frontin' like they're down with the cause
But behind the scenes
They're pulling you down with their crab claws
Be it through legislation,
Corrupted investigations,
Or trials with inadequate legal representation

So I say rise up Black Man!
Rise up and show the world
That we are taking control of our destiny
And let's vow out loud that
"I will never let them get the best of me!"
Because God is calling on us
To do our best to see a brighter day

So will you rise with me Black Man?
Will you take a stand to help claim
What is rightfully ours?
Because there aren't enough
Hours in the day for play

To be a real Black Man,
It's that ignorant,
Afraid-of-freedom mentality we must slay

So take a deep look into your eyes
And realize that it's time to rise
Just rise up brotherman and take a stand
Just rise up Black Man,
Rise UP Black Man,
Just rise up,
Rise up…

All I Want, I Now Have

I wanted a revolution
All I received is regression
I wanted social equality
All I GET is oppression

I've gone from sailing the Nile
To jailin' at Rikers Isle
All the while you laugh and smile
The way a sickly serpent would smile

I often have dreams of slaying you
But since I secretly had sentiments to become you,
I closed my 3rd eye and manipulated myself into believing
That my dreams of defiance
Were a nigga's nightmares

And I was scared to tear your heart out
Or even call you out for what you have done to me
And for what I have done to myself
...In that order

So I stopped staring at you and began to search inside me
And what I found was that the Nile never left me,
Nubia never left me,
Malcolm never left me,
The strong black woman you said did not exist,
I found her and I realized she never left me

So now even in the prison of indecision
My soul is saved
And I can get by day by day
Though I know you want to erase me,
Deface me,
Displace me

For now I know that I have a continent
And a movement called pan-Africanism
That has been waiting for my entire lifetime
To embrace me

What Are You Willing To Do For Yours?

What are you willing to do for yours?
I'm talkin' about your freedom brother, sister, "nigga," "bitch"
Whatever you call yourselves, tell me
What are you willing to do for yours?

We said that the revolution would not be televised,
But I watched the Million Man March
On CNN, C-Span, ABC and NBC
But they can't see that our revolution
Won't pause for commercial breaks and retakes
And that there will be no closed captioning
For those who refuse to hear the call to arms

There's only one bullet in the chamber of revolution
And one ballot to dispose of putrid politicians
But it's no longer a question of the ballot vs. the bullet
Because now we need the ballot and the bullet PLUS bank
Because Bill Gates owns more stock than all blacks in America
One white man owns more stock than all blacks in America

But what's the use of having the bullet if you're afraid to pull it?
If you're afraid to proudly pull the trigger
That'll turn that nigga into a real black man
Who'll stand up, throw down and die for his
So what are you willing to do for yours?

You got people in Syria stickin' swords in their stomachs
In order to show devotion to the notion of their cause
And you're sayin' you can't unite with your black woman
Because she has too many flaws

You got little kids in Vietnam
Who strapped bombs around their waists and arms
To sacrifice themselves and save their nation
And you can't get your kids off of PlayStation

You got people in China
Who stood barefoot
In front of tanks in Tiananmen Square for theirs
And you can't support your own black banks anywhere

Your own government is killin' your leaders by way of the CIA
And all you care about is gettin' home in time to see the NBA
You're killin' yourselves with pork and NutraSweet
While your brothers are being killed by that other white meat
So what the hell are you willing to do for yours?

Are you willing to pull that trigger?
You pulled the trigger in WWI, WWII,
Vietnam, Korea, the Gulf War, Iraq, and Kosovo
But when it's time to simply march for Amadou Diallo
You're a no-show

Are you willing to bleed?
You bled in their wars overseas
But you have no blood for our wars in the classroom,
Wars on the streets,
Wars in the prisons,
Or the war for your child's mind

And I haven't even told you what you HAVE to do for yours
I just asked you what you're WILLING to do for yours
What you HAVE to do is a narrative for another day

Just know that for me
I'm willing to stand up, throw down and die for mine
And I'm willing to slay you too if you get in my way
Because I realize that my enemies
Don't always have blond hair and blue eyes
And my allies don't always have nappy hair and brown eyes

But there are many ways to start a revolution
If you choose not to pull that trigger,
   Or cast that ballot,
      Or invest in some of these companies that you patronize

Reading books
Can start a revolution
Righting your wrongs
Can start a revolution
Re-writing the righteous rhythms of a people
Twice removed from their continent
Can start a revolution

131

Being committed to your black queen or king
Can start a revolution
Being consistent in your political ideology
Can start a revolution
Going to church on days other than Christmas or Easter
Can start a revolution
And learning how to read your Qu-ran in Arabic
And not European renditions
Can start a revolution

Whatever weapon you possess
You must pull that trigger
If you are to truly be free
You must find your own path
On how a revolution must start
Because it must start

All I'm asking soldier,
Is that you do your part
And commit to the cause
In mind, body, spirit, and heart
So tell me,
What are you willing to do for yours?

Big Bid'ne$$*

Je suis né
en pri$on,
Sans raison
Chaque jour,
De chaque mois,
De chaque saison,
Je reste dans une cellule de la société
Jamais, une maison

When I was a child
A news reporter once said that "Crime doesn't pay"
But there must have been a disruption in the airwaves
Or maybe I changed the channel too soon
Obviously in a rush to watch my morning cartoons

Something must have happened that day
Because now that I'm older
I realize that I didn't here him say the rest of his sentence
Because he must have said, he HAD to have said:
"Crime doesn't pay, those who are incarcerated"
Because the pri$on industrial complex
Is a multibillion dollar business

The entire system takes victims
And invests them in pri$ons
Where they accrue millions
In the interest of politicians and corporations

Government organizations like
The American Legislative Exchange Commission
Trade legislation for covert compensation
From conglomerate groups in 3-piece pursuits
To get me to spend more time for pettier crime
So they can get more loot
As they creep into every aspect of American industry

Companies like Soddexxho and Marriott,
Takin' profits off the top from cafeteria college services
All while earning a double income from inmates
Who eat from that same Soddexxho plate

So you could be getting your bachelor's degree
    Or your master's degree,
        Or your PhD,
            Or serving 25-30,
But you're eating from that same dirty system
But read closer because it's only the beginnin'

You can now buy furniture
Manufactured by pri$oners
Because pri$on labor is so diversified
That inmates don't only make license plates anymore

CEOs are so hyped up on big bucks
That they're getting ill
Waitin' on crime bills
To overfill the penitentiaries they build
On the backs of taxpayers

Private pri$on concentration camps
Are creeping up in Boston, Austin, Oakland, and DC
Waitin' for brothers and sisters like you and me
To enter that new "Door of no return"
Called the U.S. judicial system

Where federal and private buses are on highway transit,
Simulating transatlantic slave voyages with over packed cargo
While the government places embargos on family visitation
Saying that all inmates are threats to mankind
When 70% of those locked up
Haven't even committed violent crimes
Is it not time for a change
Or time to change the way we serve time?

Isn't it time for pri$oners
To no longer be paid a developing country's wage
For labor that yields billions in profits
For corporate killers of colored America?

Isn't it time for banks
To stop claiming that they build community ties
When they devilishly devise schemes
To lend and repossess people of color's American dreams
All while helping pri$ons survive with hefty loans

To better accommodate those evicted, then convicted?

Now I ain't sayin' that no one belongs behind bars
Or that violent criminals shouldn't suffer
To the fullest extent of the law

But I think it's also a crime to have NASDAQ stocks rise
As pri$on construction hits all time highs
And standardized test scores hit all time lows
Since incarceration takes precedence over educational woes

For I'm sure you didn't know that 90% of those locked up
Have no high school diploma or GED
But they must be getting some form of education
Because judges keep throwing the book at 'em

See there's something wrong
When a society seeks to incarcerate before it educates
When inmates can't vote
But their mass incarceration rates win elections for senators

Almost makes everyone locked up a political pri$oner
In the eyes of sinister civil servants
In cahoots with corporate criminals all cashing in on crime
Now who the hell's gonna prosecute that?

Well we've already started to act
By laying these corporate cops on their billionaire backs
And we may not have millions of dollars
But we have millions of misguided minds misinformed
About the pri$on system

So we're gonna teach the world about pri$on proliferation
At the expense of education & violence prevention programs
Because it's time to tell the government
That they can no longer have fun
Incarcerating our daughters and sons
Because day-by-day and one-by-one
We're going to make sure that crime really doesn't pay
ANYONE

*Partially inspired by the Prison Moratorium Project

Hi!

I have a secret
I see black people, but they don't see me
On college campuses, in the workplace
Even sometimes at the club or in the streets
I see them and I try to say "Hi"
But they turn and keep walking

It's like damn!
I'm talking and talking to them but it's an effort in futility
Because they find no utility in speaking to a brother like me
With this African jewelry and Congolese ancestry

I don't know what to do to get some attention
Because I forgot to also mention
That folks have the most creative ways of ignoring me

Some will look directly into my face and just be silent
Like I'm gonna turn violent on them if they speak

Then there are others that spot me from a distance
But then in the instance they get near me
They turn in the opposite direction
As I say "hello" to the backs of their necks
And I just wanna grab them by the throat and smack them silly
While I'm yelling at them
Like that Verizon commercial:
"Can you hear me now?"

It's like I can't get any respect from my people man
I mean damn sister,
I'm not trying to get your number or be your man
And brother,
I'm not even tryin' to shake your hand

I'm not trying to enlist you in the movement
Or turn you into a rhetorical revolutionary poet
I just want some acknowledgement from you
Because there are so few of us walkin' around in this land

So I'll be damned
If I'm gonna stop trying to speak to y'all in the streets
No matter how much better it makes you feel
When you turn the other cheek

I'm gonna get your attention
One way or another
So next time you see me in the streets,
It'll make my day if you just holla at a brother

You don't have to say "Hi" or ask me how I'm doin'
A little nod of the head is all that I'm pursuin'
All you gotta do is nod when you see me
And the rest of y'all can holla if ya hear me

Restitution

America owes us
America owes us big

Promises made
Promises not kept

Blood, sweat, and tears
Yes, our ancestors wept
As their masters crept
Into their shacks and violated our women
For that sugar sweet but savage
And "unsaved" molasses
Making them true believers in the "one true God"
By the proselytizing penis process

Yes, America owes us
And we're all too willing to take

We believe that reparations are our key to paradise
But we must think twice
We must realize that the more others give us
The more we forget about ourselves

We have been living for over 500 years
In a spiritual coma
And now we believe some cash
Will cure us of our historical glaucoma

We must have forgotten
That our emancipation was proclaimed in 1863
But our African identity began to fade
Before the turn of that century

We must have forgotten
That we earned the right to vote
For too many of us choose not to go to the polls
And pick our politicians with pride

We earned our "civil" rights in 1965
But black-on-black crime
Is still one of our biggest obstacles
To keeping our youth alive

Affirmative action affirmed the assumption
That black individual flight
Would lead the greater black community
Into economic and political plight

You can count black-owned businesses
In the 'hood on one hand
But rather than take a stand you'd rather stick out your hand
For a paycheck for a past you've forgotten!

You don't know our liberators like Garvey and Nat Turner
But it's okay as long as you get that PlayStation
…and CD burner
For centuries of enslavement and murder?

What's next,
Forget about Dr. King and Malcolm X
On our quest for 40 acres, a mule
And a Lexus?

Let us work towards spiritual liberation
Before financial compensation
Let us tell the world our story
Before we are slapped into further silence
By the hand we're still begging to feed us

Our future seeds need us
To ensure their culture is preserved

Let us turn the world right side up
With our economic might
Let us withhold our dollars
From those who are cultural robbers

Let us not buy from our oppressors,
Those who built their universities, corporations
And the entire nation on our backs

YES,
America owes us
But we're not mentally ready to receive

If reparations will lead to more materialistic gain
But leave our schools in academic disdain
If it will buy us a Lexus
But make us forget about
400 years of cultural, political, and religious rape
Then I would tell the United States
To keep her money in the bank

But if reparations will be used
To re-Africanize our Eurocentric system of education,
If it will not further divide us
Into African vs. West Indian vs. African American,
If it will allow us the liberty to create institutions
That show us how to keep our dollars in the community,
Then I say YES to reparations
But think about what you're asking?

You expect those who have forced your mother Africa
To abort more than 100 million of her children
And miscarriage the minds of countless others
To fix our predicament?
You expect those who have taken your language
To stop your anguish?

Do you expect misappropriated reparations
Will really uplift the greater black American nation?
Do you think our bliss will trickle down
Like Reagan Economics
From the hand that you're begging to feed you?

Realize that you keep eating from that hand
Because his food is laced

With an anti-revolution sedative
And this diet has been repetitive
For hundreds of years

The struggle needs to now focus
On a spiritual revolution
And not financial restitution

If we can show the world
That we have healed ourselves
By putting our color, class,
And political issues on the shelves

If we show the world how withholding our money
Can cripple a world economy
And if we could spit rhymes that show the world
That we see our skin as divine donation from above
Then no form of reparations will replace
Our freshly found affluence of self love

As other people who have
Received reparations have shown,
True reparations come to those
Who first take care of home

Bush-whacked

I

For Bush, you are the WTO
Worthless **T**eenage **O**nlookers with no influence on his policies
You are the IMF
Immature **M**ales & **F**emales
With no notion of the world overseas
You are his domestic UN
Uninformed **N**eophytes, partying all night under neon lights

You voting him out of office
Would be the decisive definition of a Patriot Act
Election day is on hope's horizon
Will you authoritatively act or wait four more years to re-act?

II

While you try to build international walls
Of peace, prosperity and progress
Your president has written you off as "Generation Worthless"
His evangelical is quite identical to dictators of past times
And since he does not respect your minds
Half the world now hates your American kind
If America is really the land of the free
Why won't you vote and liberate yourself
From Ignorance's policies?

III

Mr. President promotes policies
That put all American people in peril
Preventing the peace process
Through preemptive propaganda
Is an act most feral
We're too busy trying to demonstrate
But we can't even regulate the air that we breathe
And his patriotic acts got us watchin' our backs
And scared for what we read
But we gotta forget our fear
And organize while he tries to globalize

Because we cannot let him succeed!

IV

Daughter asks:
Daddy, why do you vote?

Father replies:
Baby, society seeks satiation from the milk of human kindness
Bush spouts "no child left behind"
But cuts on educational spending
Have left too many of our nation's future on the sidelines

Daughter asks:
But Daddy, why are **you** so vigorous on voting,
Especially this time?

Father replies:
Baby,
I vote so that you claim your rightful place
In the framing of our future's frontline

WHAT?

Deep isn't when you don't get your check on Friday
Deep isn't how you try to opine
In front of impressionable minds
In the school cafeteria

Deep is what our ancestors are
At the bottom of the Atlantic
Having jumped overboard slave ships
With their babies in a panic

What you are is shallow
Shallow like going to Sunday service in a limo
Shallow like saying you can't unite with your brother
Because he's a homo...sexuality is a reality
Don't matter how a brother dies
It's another uncalled for fatality

Morality what?
You deem it moral to quarrel
About Malcolm as our leader vs. Martin instead?
When they were both shot down dead in the head?

Do you think the government cared
Or compared Christianity vs. Islam?
As long as one led us to our freedom
It was wrong

What's more insane
Is that they both died in vain
We went from makin' it plain
To thinkin' we keepin' it real

They've been killin' our minds
By committing the crime
Called eurocentric education
Grades K through 9

While we singin' hip-hop songs
They're droppin' academic napalm bombs

In our schools
Turning our young great black minds
Into whitewashed fools

Why haven't YOU gone back to your school
Since you graduated?
What?
Are you emancipated?

I'm not fascinated by your degrees
Negro please!
You caught that disease called
"Iwenttotheirschoolssoi'mbetterthanyou" fever
While neither you nor your degree
Has made us anymore free

Got your PhD in Socrates
But didn't learn that we invented philosophy?
What good are you to me
As a soldier in their army?

You need to shut up fool
And get to work on the struggle
And stop digging us deeper into oblivion
With that shovel you call your tongue

Stop sellin' us out on every occasion
And tryin' to show them
That under that beautiful, bold,
Yet beleaguered black skin
Is a wannabe Caucasian

Embrace who you are
And be proud of your African self
And your inferiority complex
Will take care of itself

...Is Like a Tree Without Roots"
- MARCUS GARVEY

Rhyming With History

Truman once said
That the only thing new in this world
Is the history you do not know

Mark Twain once said
That history does not repeat itself
But it rhymes

Put both testimonies together,
And it means that
Those who do not understand their history
Might be doomed to rhyme with it

Now when I say "rhyming"
I'm talking about like how unpopular presidents
Start wars with perfect timing
Whenever they hear their popularity is sliding
And so history rhymes

From civilizing missions to colonization
To international development it rhymes
From the Plague to AIDS it rhymes
Like endless cycles of genocide
From Armenia to Germany
And from Rwanda to Congo it rhymes
From Jewish to Japanese concentration camps it rhymes
From Gas ovens in Auschwitz to gas chambers
For falsely convicted felons it rhymes

Like Palestinians and so-called Indians
Trying to reclaim their land it rhymes
From regime change in Iraq and Haiti it rhymes
From disgruntled former United States employees
Now despising America—Saddam to Osama
O-soma y'all forget that rhymes

From liberators like L'Ouverture and Lumumba
Turning down Western bribes it rhymes
Unfortunately the states of their countries also rhyme
But that'll hopefully change for the better in time

Why can't you see that it all rhymes!

Like going from Native Americans and smallpox
To Tuskegee experiments with syphilis
From African rebel leaders becoming members of government
By maiming their way into office
From Thomas Jefferson to Strom Thurman's
Black and kept-in-the-closet children,
From Lincoln to Kennedy,
And from Malcolm to Martin to Medgar,

From Emmitt Till to Marcus Dixon,
From Charles Stuart to Susan Smith,
From black niggas to sand niggas in America,
From male CEOs to male politicians
Both believing a women's place
Isn't at the table but on the table,

From liberal republicans to conservative democrats,
From Condoleezza Rice to Janet Jackson
Serving as history's scapegoats,
From Elvis to Eminem,
And from rock & roll to rap music, it Mos Def-initely rhymes

From Kobe to MJ—I mean OJ, it rhymes
From Madame CJ Walker to Oprah it rhymes
Hell, from Richard Pryor to Dave Chappelle, it rhymes

From Alvin Ailey to Shaumba-Yandje
Creating opportunities for colored kids it rhymes
From Jews in ancient Egypt
To blacks in modern day America it rhymes
But this time,
We gonna let our own people go
'Cause we ain't askin' no mo'

History just rhymes and rhymes
Like how behind every great fortune,
There's a crime
And it could be from the late Frank Sinatra
To the late Frank White
But the lyrics are the same

Whether it's from Steppin' Fetchit to Sleep & Eat
Or from Amos & Andy to New Millennium Minstrel shows
From "Birth of a Nation" to "Soul Plane" it rhymes

'Cause both films show blacks
Incapable of properly running businesses
From governments to airlines

From Tammi Terrell to Minnie Riperton,
And from Aaliyah to Left Eye
Dying before their time it rhymes
From Sam Cooke to Marvin Gaye
And from Tupac to Notorious B.I.G. it rhymes
So is a change gon' come?

I keep reading history and it almost always rhymes
Though I'm still waiting
For Milosevic and Kagame to rhyme
As it relates to being tried for war crimes

And I'm still waiting
For Jewish and Japanese reparations
To rhyme with black subjugation
But I know it'll happen in time

And I'm hoping that saying these lines
Won't cause me to rhyme
With assassination attempts on my father
But we'll only know in due time

You must know that there's
Nothing new under the sun
So find your place in time
Look back in historical rhymes
And see what group or people
Your predicament rhymes with

See whose style you're biting
Whose history you're co-writing
And learn from the mistakes of past peoples
Before you run out of time

Because the only thing new in this world
Is the history you do not know
And history doesn't repeat itself,
It rhymes

A Daughter's Cry In The Black Man's Destiny

If it wasn't for you, I wouldn't be here
At night I count on you to take away my fears
I need you here to build a strong foundation
Soon we won't be able to build a strong black nation

At night, I talk to "Martin," MTV, and BET
You know lonely children find best friends in TV
Momma's tryin', but she can't do it alone
Because society is removing black queens from their thrones

Where are you Daddy?
Is your job so important?
Is your car so beautiful,
That instead of me, you flaunt it?

What has this society done to you?
These ways of the West
Why do they engulf you
Make you treat me so less?

You're treating me worth less than what I am,
A young queen in the making
When you tell me you "love" me
I feel that you're faking!

This world has raped me
Of my culture and my history
And now I'm looking to you
To put an end to my misery

But Daddy I'm looking
Can you make yourself present?
Did you stop loving and caring
Once Mommy got pregnant?

Don't you love me father?
Don't you love your own daughter?
Can you come back home
To me and Momma?

Don't let them fool you
Money can't raise a people
Without ME, Black Father,
Our race has no sequel

So please Black Father
I need you and Ma' needs you too
Yes, take charge of your destiny
But please take us with you

This Could Be Your Child

I love my father
I respect my father
But I dare not tell him
I'm scared to tell him

Will I be rejected or scorned?
How does he feel?
What I'd give to know
He never told me what he thought of me

Does he care?
Does he regret having me?
How do I know what's right and wrong?
Why won't he talk to me more?

Should I smoke?
Cut school?
Stay in school?
I'm only in the eighth grade

Wait,
Maybe if I talk to them,
Them on that corner,
The right decision will be made

Don't Talk To Strangers*

When I was a child,
I was told to never talk to strangers
I was told that if someone confronts me who I do not know
That I should run in the opposite direction
But where did I run to?
With parental permission of course,
I ran straight to the television
Where there are more strangers than you find in the streets

Through television
I allowed these strangers to creep into my mind
As have countless other young black males over the years

These "celebrity strangers"
Disguised as black men
Showed me how to do everything
But be a real black man

These illegal black male aliens
From Martin Lawrence to Jaime Foxx
And countless others over the years
Have proudly dressed as women
At some point in their Steppin' Fetchit careers
Proudly serving to destroy the image
Of the strong black male
In this young black mind

So as me and my brethren
Went from Kyle Barker to Jay-Z
We learned to become players
And aspiring rhyme-sayers

Our luminescent thoughts of revolution
Quickly grew dim
When we watched repeats of
"Men on Film" with Damon Wayans

Our aspirations of liberation
Quickly come to an end
When we watched

Racial profiling skits on "Girlfriends"

Our high hopes for racial equality
Quickly fell deeper
When we saw Ray-J being
Arrested on "Moesha"

And why haven't you realized
That our children are becoming more violent
When they're sat down in front of famous strangers
In order to be kept silent!

And if you choose to ignore this fact
And stand idly by
Then realize you're serving
As an accessory to mental and generational genocide

And as far as the sitcom producers care
The death of our minds,
That is an acceptable casualty
As long as their ratings rise dramatically

I know that from now on
Before I see a child
Turning on Fox & Warner Bros.
I'm gonna have to warn-a-brother:

The contents you are about to see
Are solely intended to convince you
That you are not strong
And that unity with your black woman
Can only come in a physical, sexual manner
These sitcoms are psychological time bombs
That when detonated
Will send you back to school
Dressed with the newest knowledge
Of how to act a fool
And still be considered cool
Because all of your peers aspire to be like you too
Now if you can also turn on your PlayStation
And create your own society
That centers around a circus of violence
Now by your 18th birthday,

*You may not know how to spell
But hell,
You'll know the secret codes
To NBA Live, NFL Blitz, and Tekken 4 all too well
Now people may say this is not the way
But your parents bought you that PlayStation
For your 13th birthday
SO IT'S ALL OK*

TV glorifies sex, violence,
And the destruction of the young black mind

The next time you choose
To silence your young Shaka Zulu in the making
Sit him down in front of images of Dr. King
Or play him speeches by brother Malcolm

Give him coloring books
That showcase black greatness
And not BET images
Of confused black men

Remember,
Just because it was a black-owned station
Doesn't mean its overall goal
Is to uplift the nation

If our children cannot
Turn to our adults to find peace
Then our hopes of finding black manhood
And attaining liberation
Will forever rest in peace
So remember, don't talk to strangers

Partially inspired by Shaka Washington

Take My Hand

I am the proud product
Of thousands of years of civilizations
The seed of great nations and generations
My OrigiNation is your destination

I'm trying to make a name on an insane plane
Where children are to be seen, beaten, raped and molested
But not heard
This is absurd

I'm the victimized voice of your clouded conscious
The carrier of your ancestry
I should be respected like your humble highness
Or a young majesty

I'm the one you should be teachin'
While you're preachin'
To the masses
...Reachin' no one

I'm your son,
Your daughter
The fragile fruit
Of our forgotten forefathers

Believe in me
Invest in me
Tell me you love me
...Before that gang does

What was your seed
Is now a flourishing flower
Thirsting for the water
That is your love,
Love, LOVE ME!
Love me like you loved creating me

This world is degrading
And berating me
For problems I don't even understand

Can you save me?

Love me now
Or lament losing me later
The choice is yours

I am nothing without you
But with you
I am any and everything

Help me become what I was intended to be
The son of longevity,
The daughter of eternity

Take my hand and show me the way,
And I promise tomorrow will be a better day

LOVE ME

POUR LES FRANCOPHONES

Justice
(Ecrit avant le 11 septembre 2001)

Je viens d'une terre privée de liberté par le pays de la liberté
Depuis plus de 140 ans, Amérique, tes cousins Belges et toi
Commettaient des crimes dans mon Congo
Tels que couper les bras de mon peuple
Parce que n'ayant pas assez produit
De caoutchouc pour Dunlop
Sans bras, comment arrive t-on à reconstruire une nation ?

10 millions d'âmes ont péri entre 1885 et 1910
Et toi Amérique tu assistait à ce génocide
Les Belges et toi, aviez partagé votre tarte congolaise en 1885
Et je n'ai toujours pas eu ma part du gâteau américain

Nous étions ton orifice africain
Que l'oncle Sam sodomisait pour ses ressources naturelles
Tout en avalant la souillante et sinistre semence
Du pénis du Roi Léopold
Tu ricanais lorsque les Belges prenaient en otage nos femmes
Pour nous obliger à travailler
Sans procréation, comment peut-on reconstruire une nation ?

Quand les Belges nous «gratifiaient» de l'indépendance
Nous n'avions qu'un seul diplômé dans tout le pays
Sans instruction – nul n'enseigne à personne
Comment peut-on reconstruire une nation ?

Amérique,
Le sang de mon peuple congolais bien-aimé est sur tes mains
N'essaie pas de le nier
Ce caoutchouc rouge dégouline de tes doigts et canines

Alors, tu veux que je compatisse
Pour Columbine ?
Tu veux que je compatisse
Pour les actes de Timothy McVeigh ?

Je n'éprouve aucune sympathie pour toi Amérique
Parce que tu n'as pas encore réalisé
Que quand tu sèmes l'oppression

Tu la moissonnes toi-même

Depuis que voue êtes arrivés, les arabes et toi
Mon peuple n'a plus jamais connu de liberté
Alors que toi, tu jouis de toute ta liberté

A présent,
Tu es en colère pour tous les dégâts que tu as commis
Qui, de partout dans le monde te retombent sur la face
N'en veux pas à moi, à ton frangin ou ton gouvernement
Prends toi à Dieu, parce que Lui est juste
Tout ce que Dieu procure c'est la justice

...Et pourtant, je ne connais même pas son nom

(Une histoire authentique)

Saviez vous que j'ai théorisé la conspiration ?
En fait, je suis encore théoricien de la conspiration
J'ai comploté à propos de tout
Depuis les pilules contraceptive du Ku Klux Klan
Dans le poulet aux hormones
Jusqu'à ce qui a conduit les enfants à qui j'ai enseigné
A se mettre au Ridlin
J'ai foi dans presque tous les complots visant
A éliminer les leaders noirs
De Shaca Zulu à Patrice Lumumba, du Docteur King
Jusqu'aux plus récents
Je donne aussi mon avis sur la fabrication du SIDA
Dans les laboratoires occidentaux
Pour enrailler les peuples noirs du monde

Mais j'ai réalisé que mes théories sur les complots
Ont peu d'effet
Parce que ma Cousine, en Zambie, meurt du SIDA
Et je ne connais même pas son nom

Penser que le SIDA provient des homosexuels
Marginaux ou du rhésus de singes
Dans les laboratoires américaines n'aide pas
Ma cousine à assister à son prochain anniversaire
Ou à celui de son enfant

C'est fou de penser à ces morts insensées
Causées par cette maladie aux origines,
Entre guillemets, inconnues
Bien sûr que çà s'empire, à présent qu'elle est à nos portes

J'ai souvent pensé à ma cousine
Et comment elle a perdu son époux
Avec cette faucheuse macabre de SIDA
Mais lorsque j'approfondis ma pensée
Et vois qu'il est mort parce que face au choix
Acheter les médicaments coûteux ou nourrir ces enfants
A présent qu'ils meurent de faim, sa mort a été vaine

...Et dire que je ne connais même pas son nom

Les firmes américaines du médicament
Ne baisseront pas le prix de leurs remèdes
Alors à son tour d'attendre la mort dans l'indigence et
l'avilissement
...Et dire que je ne connais même pas son nom
Plus d'école pour ses fils
...Et dire que je ne connais même pas son nom
Sa fille pourrait être enlevée
Par des bandes d'hommes infectés,
En quête futile de remèdes contre leur mal
...Et dire que je ne connais même pas son noms
Ses enfants mourront certainement
A cause de ce jeu abominable livré
Autour du médicament américain
...Et dire que je ne connais même pas son nom
Ma cousine se meurt du SIDA
Et je ne connais même pas son nom!

Cela pourrait paraître un leitmotiv,
Mais dans sa vie entière, tout a été négatif
Et maintenant la voilà positive du SIDA
Je sens qu'avant qu'elle ne disparaisse,
Je dois rattraper le temps perdu
Dans les statistiques d'Africains mourant de SIDA
De paludisme, de tuberculose ou d'un banal rhume
Tant que nous ne connaissons pas leur nom
Et que la plupart des américains croient
Que tous les africains sont pareils
A moins qu'ils ne meurent de guerre ou famine,
Ils périront tous du SIDA
Mais pas de vieillesse ni de rage, même les nouveaux nés
Ils crèveront tous de cette maladie que nous nommons SIDA

Au fait, qui connaît ce « SIDA » ?
Certains disent qu'il s'agit
Du Syndrome d'Immunodéficience Acquise
Mais en réalité il pourrait être
le Syndrome Inventé pour la Déchéance des Africains
Parce que nul ne se soucie réellement de leur nom,
N'est-ce pas ?

Archi faux!
Désormais je vais entonner la chanson de ma cousine
Le cantique de ces foules qui meurent en si grand nombre
En autant de nouvelles rivières de larmes qui ne sèchent pas
Entretenues par la multitude de victimes du SIDA
Je vais demeurer fort pour ma cousine
Afin de combattre pour elle et son mari

L'impossibilité de payer le prix exorbitant
De ces médicaments de marque
Signifie que ma cousine va mourir dans la déchéance
Au moins pour cette âme, la mort ne sera pas vaine
Parce qu'il est temps d'entendre son témoignage
Je connaîtrai son nom

Son nom n'est pas le numéro 10 000 001
Sur les statistiques africaines
Ou un quelconque chiffre
Qui enrichira davantage les firmes pharmaceutiques
Je dirai en même temps à mes amis
Que plaisanter avec la SIDA n'a jamais été
Et ne sera jamais drôle

Si vous ou eux me demandent la raison
Je leur dirais alors que ma cousine Kuishi* se meurt du SIDA
Malgré que certains d'entre vous
Ne se soucient guère de ceux dont ils ont la charge
Je vous prie de vous joindre à moi
Pour un moment de recueillement à l'intension de Kuishi

*Kuishi – « Vivre » en Swahili

Souffle de la mère patrie

Un livre ne s'apprécie guère par sa couverture, disent-ils
Mais ils admettent qu'un continent soit apprécié
A partir de sa représentation médiatique
Avec les pinceaux de la perception débile,
Peut être peint en noir, tout un continent
Dès lors qu'on compte sur les médias
Pour renseigner sur l'Afrique

Je viens d'un continent qu'on croit n'être qu'un pays
Et plus, tous séropositifs, sommes-nous présumés,
Jusqu'à preuve du contraire
A croire que l'Afrique est plutôt un immense Safari ou Kalahari,
Bouillonnant de paganisme
Dépourvu de religion, berceau de bestialité et d'animisme
La misère africaine à travers la télévision,
Renvoie à une terre de sauvages
Au sein de laquelle les pires maux défient la loi de l'équilibre
La télévision, en Amérique ne montre
Que la déchéance de pays bien ciblés
Les américains, alors juxtaposent mère civilisation
Avec les expressions telles que damnation et famine
Sans contrôle sur notre image
Point d'espoir de voir la beauté véritable de notre visage

La seule grande contribution de l'Afrique se limite
A des expressions comme
« Hakuna Matata », « Asante sana squash banana »,
Outre les sites de vacances exotiques et reculés;
Telle est leur conviction de non africains
D'aucune télévision américaine
J'ai entendu dire que nous sommes constitués
De plus de 54 nations

Pour ces medias
Nous sommes juste des spécimens sous développés
En quête de civilisation
Ai-je besoin de poursuivre si déjà tu acceptes l'image
Qu'ils se font de nous, ces medias ?
Le pire,
C'est WB, ABC, NBC,

Redoutables armes de destruction de la conscience
Ils ne voient que ce que leur projette cette astucieuse bombe
Qu'est la television

Ces non africains
Et pas seulement à travers les actualités
Cela commence très tôt, dès à peine l'âge de trois ans
J'ai grandi avec les images de Bugs Bunny à la face nègre
Vêtu de paille et s'exprimant en dialecte africain
Et à chaque décennie sa nouvelle version de Tarzan
Je revois les africains tel que représentés
Dans ces dessins animés de TINTIN
Et lorsque ôté le casque aux airs loufoques de Marvin Martian
Il se révèle un africain dégénéré, perfide,
Ravagé par la faim, au ventre ballonnant

Voilà les stéréotypes du contexte
Qui a donné naissance aux politiciens
Dont l'opinion sur notre patrie est bâtie à partir de films
surannés tels « Congo », « Les gorilles en plein dans le milieu »,
et « Du vent par là »
Nous ne saurions oublier « Les larmes du soleil »
Qui ont laissé en larmes nombre de fils et filles d'Afrique
Cherchant la belle image de notre patrie

Vains seraient les efforts,
Si les africains ne prennent aucune responsabilité
Car, l'aversion de nos amis de FOX, CBS et CNN
C'est voir cesser ces caricatures
Du continent mère de l'humanité
Plutôt dépeint comme son mouroir, prêt pour la crémation
Montrons au monde entier
Que notre mère Afrique est forte, pétillante et défiante
Parce que le souffle de plus d'un milliard d'âmes ne peut
S'éteindre lorsque nous avons le contrôle
De ce qui est montré au monde
Ne soyons pas complices de ces sombres dessins
De notre patrie
Peints à travers la télévision, par des pessimistes

Parce que nous sommes le souffle de la mère patrie
Et fiers, nous nous dresserons face au monde

Vie privatisée

Pendant que vous lirez ce témoignage
17 enfants seront morts à travers le monde
Huit enfants meurent toutes les minutes,
A la recherche d'eau potable
Face à ces morts de femmes et d'hommes,
Vous finirez par maudire vos yeux
Ces morts tout évitables soient-elles
Vont s'accroître, parce que l'eau est privatisée

Repu du monopole sur le diamant, l'or, le charbon et le bétail
L'homme s'arroge la mission
De monopoliser l'âme de Mère Nature
Plus possible de nager et boire aux affluents
Des deltas du monde
Le prix de cette eau nourricière
Est à payer pour se soustraire des pages nécrologiques
Les Programmes d'ajustement structurel
Sont synonymes de privation
Nos gouvernements parmi les plus pauvres au monde
Doivent privatiser l'eau
Pour honorer ces dettes éternelles

L'AGOA est rabougri par les mesures les plus tyranniques
Tandis que les entreprises commerciales
S'arrachent le droit à l'eau
Dans une panique, style conférence de Berlin

Les droits humains et à la Terre perdent toute pertinence
En faveur du droit au profit, désormais mis en avant
Ne tarderont plus à suivre
Le standard minimum d'accès à l'eau
Et le tarissement des réserves
Puisque la Terre mère devient le Mars de demain,
Dépourvu de liquide

Du sang des diamants au sang de l'eau,
L'histoire lorgne de son troisième œil
Nous mettant en garde contre l'imminence
D'un affrontement indéniable
Des guerres civiles seront menées

Au nom de la course gratuite vers l'eau du monde
Réveillant des réminiscences de conflits
Dans le genre des massacres de nos jours

Le monde développé,
Très souvent agit selon des méthodes les plus archaïques
Misant sur la survie des plus pauvres
De la protection des intérêts des entreprises capitalistes
A l'ensevelissement des dépouilles des cadavres

Les IFI ont intégré l'industrialisation de nos ressources naturelles
Cependant,
Nombre d'entre nous combattra
Et désormais de manière ouverte
Nous n'admettrons jamais
Que les ressources de notre Terre nourricière soient brevetées

En tant que « carburant » de l'homme
Dans ce nouveau millénaire
Les plus pauvres parmi les pauvres accrocheront leur vie
Sur la pendule du profit
Demeurer inactif c'est militer en faveur de la privatisation
Et de la destruction de l'homme

Alors le sang des 17 enfants qui viennent de mourir
Coulent aussi sur vos mains

Libère ton esprit africain

Libère ton esprit, mon frère
Libère ton esprit, ma sœur,
De ces chaînes, libère-toi
Elles te font croire que d'un «obscure continent», tu es issu
Pourtant sur ce continent, tu ne vois personne plus noir que toi

Tu as été endoctriné par le Blanc malicieux
Et tes frangins aussi ont contribué à ton aliénation
Exténuants ont été les viols, pendaisons et castrations
Mais la castration de l'esprit
Marque plus profondément qu'un lynchage

De la terre mère tu t'éloignes de plus en plus
Ils te font croire que ton parlé
Inspiré de l'esclavage, est plutôt indigène
Et non une riche langue africaine,
Agrémentée de mots d'anglais
Au point que tu aies honte de la parler

Tu les crois quand ils disent que l'Afrique est ténébreuse,
Et pourtant, tu n'en savais rien
Parce que pendant des siècles,
Ils ont essayé de dérober sa lueur

En blanchissant l'Égypte ancienne, Beethoven,
Et Michael Jackson
Ils t'ont endoctriné
Des codes de l'esclavage,
Aux codes des noirs en passant par le code de Jim Crow
Ils t'ont endoctriné
De K-1 aux louanges,
Tu as été endoctriné

Alors que l'Amérique a décidé de ne plus avoir besoin de toi
Tu veux devenir américain
Et pourtant un continent tout entier
Te supplie de rentrer au bercail
Libère ton esprit africain, te dis-je

Libère ce que en toi, le système a endormi

Libère ces hanches de ces jeans serrés
Qui ne font qu'attirer des regards mal intentionnés
Et étouffent tes courbes nilotiques, naturelles
Libère ces lèvres brunes et alléchantes,
De ce ravissant rouge à lèvres
Libère tes reins des quarante et déguste
Cette eau fraîche du bassin du Nil
Libère toi de l'idée de passer outre ta dame
Et d'escalader avec moi le Mont Kilimandjaro
Libère ton esprit
Et cesse de te reposer sur ton prochain
Dans notre lutte pour la liberté

Nier ton africanité c'est renier ta place de premier sur terre
Alors que tu peux te prévaloir de la Nubie ancienne
Pourquoi clamer ta négritude et tuer à un coin de rue ?
Alors que tu peux prétendre à un continent,
Pourquoi revendiquer un pays

Je m'adresse à tous ceux d'entre vous qui renient
Que tu sois Africain américain, indien de l'Ouest, Capverdien
Ou de l'Afrique continentale
Malcom et Marcus ont payé de leur vie pour libérer ton esprit

Unissons nos efforts tant qu'il est temps
Etre fier de ton sang africain fera
De toi majoritaire niveau mondial
Et non plus minoritaire à l'échelle d'un pays
Ton histoire alors s'étendra, aussi long que le Mississippi
Tu comprendras pourquoi tu es aussi beau
Pourquoi tu es fidèle à tes dévotions comme nul autre
Pourquoi tu ne peux jamais être défait
Quand tu t'en remets à Dieu et aux ancêtres

Alors tous, levez-vous
Levez-vous, prisonniers du ghetto
Qui êtes en réalité des princes du Ghana
Vous princesse du Burundi, à tord qualifiées de garces
Vous qui pensez qu'il suffit de naître
Sur le continent pour être africain
Toi...
Egocentrique eurafricain,
Amnésique Afro-asiatique,

Latino à la peau sombre
Cape verdien embarassé
Indien de l'ouest occidentalisé
Aborigène à moitié décimé
Lève-toi

Prends conscience qu'être Africains c'est un état d'esprit
Alors marche à mes côtés vers la lueur
De l'aube africaine naissante
Je suis sûr que ton âme, corps, esprit et nation se dresseront
Aussi haut que les cieux scintillants
Libère ton esprit africain tout-puissant

Le cri d'un orphelin

Voilà le cri d'un orphelin de Mbuji Mayi
C'est le cri d'un enfant
Versant des larmes sur son parent massacré
C'est le cri d'un enfant qui voit sa mère violée,
Puis sauvagement abattue par un gang
En attendant, horrifié, son tour

C'est le cri d'un orphelin
C'est le cri d'un enfant qui se demande
Où il prendrait sont repas du lendemain
Car il n'y a plus de parent pour dire «c'est prêt»

C'est le cri de l'herbe piétinée
Par deux éléphants combattants
C'est le cri d'un enfant qui voit son père tué
Et qui est exaspéré du fait
Que son frère sera bientôt le prochain

C'est le cri d'un enfant qui n'a pas espoir en l'avenir
Parce qu'il ne peut envisager le futur sans peine

C'est le cri d'un orphelin!
C'est le cri d'un enfant sachant qu'il est condamné à mort
Tout en se demandant « Pourquoi » ?

C'est le cri d'un enfant regardant les balles,
Au lieu des oiseaux, voler dans son ciel

C'est le cri d'un enfant voyant ses parents
Sauvagement abattus à Mbuji Mayi

C'est le cri d'un enfant
Qui sait que ce sera bientôt son tour... de mourir

Partout et nulle part à la fois

Congo dans notre console de jeu
Congo dans nos téléphones cellulaires
Congo dans nos avions
Congo dans nos navettes spatiales
Congo dans nos ordinateurs
Congo dans nos fourneaux
Congo, partout et nulle part à la fois
Parce que Congo n'est pas dans nos esprits

Bienvenue au Congo

Mon Congo bien aimé, la farce du continent
Le monde de l'or, du diamant et des minerais
Concubine du Rwanda
Mon propre pays,
Empoisonné par ce salaud de politique américaine

Occidentaux et Asiatiques exploitent les richesses
Laissant derrière eux des communautés cloîtrées
Avec une sécurité congolaise mal payés
Ainsi, d'une main, sur des visages fracturés,
Ils fermèrent la porte
Tout en, de l'autre main, leur dérobant leurs ressources
Et n'épargnant aucune province
Puisque certains de nos propres dirigeants
Congolais corrompus sont impliqués

Alors qu'ils ne peuvent point faire fière allure
Face à nos agresseurs rwandais
Qui ont annexé notre esprit à leur âme malade et sinistre
Au point que pour joindre l'Est du Congo, on compose
l'indicatif du Rwanda
Pendant qu'ils nourrissent l'idée
D'introduire la monnaie rwandaise à l'Est

Les Nations Unies parlent de paix
Sachant pertinemment que la paix
Ne peut être acquise sans violence
Jean Pierre Bemba
Ne peut être nommé Premier ministre sans **violence**
Des enfants soldats combattant dans la peur
De représailles sur leur famille
S'enfoncent dans le cercle vicieux de la **violence**
Violer ma Terre Mère
Et verser son sang noir ne peut continuer qu'avec la **VIOLENCE**
Et quand je parle du génocide congolais
Perpétré avec la complicité des occidentaux
Tu réponds par ...**Silence** !

Je sais; parce que j'étais comme toi
Rester là à sourire tandis que le peuple était massacré

A couvrir ma femme de diamant et pour y parvenir
Probablement verser le sang d'un cousin lointain
Choisir pour cela de l'ignorer

Maintenant que j'ai visité des camps de réfugiés congolais
Je vois qu'il n'y a point de refuse pour les réfugiés
Des mères et enfants abandonnés
Vivent sous des tentes faites de sacs de riz vides
Pendant que les cheveux infestés de poux,
Leurs filles vivent le désespoir
Ayant enfanté à 12 ans
Avec des hommes de 50 ans déjà mariés
Et dépourvus d'humilité
Qui pour leur virginité payent 25 cents
Dans l'espoir de guérir du SIDA
Pendant que la Banque Mondiale
Octroie une aide au gouvernement sans paternité

Je suis à la recherche d'un remède pour tous ces maux
Car quatre millions de personnes sont mortes en quatre années
Trop d'orphelins pleurent et meurent dans la rue,
A peine âgés de onze ans
Même s'il fait chaud, dans leur coeur ils ont froid
Errant dans une ville affamée où rares dans les rues bitumées

Un demi repas par jour ne saurait suffire pour y remédier
Des familles entières avec juste moins d'un dollar par mois
Non plus ne sauraient y remédier
Depuis, on ne voit que des images d'Israël,
D'Afghanistan et de la Palestine…
C'est inacceptable!

J'ai espoir qu'une centaine de mots vaudra une image
Les images du Congo
Ne conviendraient pas à vos estomacs, mais couvriront…
Vos doits, de diamants,
Vos oreilles, d'or,
Vos téléphones cellulaires, de coltan
Et le pétrole congolais, nouvellement découvert
Réchauffe vos maisons, quand il fait froid

Tout cela n'émeut guère
Même lorsque je parle des congolais atteints de polio

Marchant la main droite appuyée
Au genou comme s'ils étaient collés

Il existe des remèdes contre la rougeole ou le paludisme
Mais rien, contre la misère
Dans un pays sur la mauvaise pente
Avec des enfants mourants de divers types d'infection
Des filles de douze ans condamnées à la mort
Parce que des hommes riches ont fait fi du préservatif
Et finissent par être rejetées de tous
C'est comme si le pays tout entier
Avait subi une piqûre mortelle
Cela va sans dire qu'un autre génocide est à prévoir
Dans moins de cent ans
Du fait que nous sommes restés douze années sans élections
Dans cette rue congolaise dénommée « l'avenue du futur »
Mon père fut torturé et faillit mourir en détention
Vous m'excuserez alors quand je dis qu'aux yeux du peuple,
Notre avenir parait compromis

Je suis également ahuri lorsqu'ils disent
« Vive le Congo indépendant »
Je ne me souviens pas qu'il l'ait été
La communauté internationale condamne parfaitement
La corruption au Congo
En se demandant avec quoi les ministres
Achètent leurs voitures
Le monde devient sourd
Quand je demande
D'où viennent les armes de nos envahisseurs

De tout cela,
Le Congo n'en n'a cure et je ne trouve pas ça amusant
Les américains disent que c'est un endroit juste pour s'enrichir
Les alliés de bush ou de Ben Laden
Pillent les ressources de ce pays
A travers les réseaux libanais
Vivant dans un pays frappé
De sanctions internationales pour génocide
Au moment où pathétiques Etats Unies,
Plus politique putride des Nations unies égale pesticide

Ils prétendent avoir enfin apporté la paix

Ne te laisse pas embobiner
Car jusqu'aujourd'hui,
Nous déterrons encore des corps à Bunia,
Enroulés dans des sacs

Leur rôle au Congo ne va pas plus qu'attiser la violence
Notre quête effrénée de trésors congolais
Qui n'ont jamais profités aux masses - Complicité
Des expériences effectuées sur des Congolais bien portants
Avec des médicaments contre le Sida
Non encore testés – au nom de la science
Des poèmes comme celui-ci
Pour tenter de nous ouvrir les yeux –
Un simple acte de défiance
Tout ce que je demande
Pour mon peuple congolais bien aimé: une confiance en soi
Et lorsque je te demande de m'aider
A panser le cœur meurtri de l'Afrique
Tu réponds par ...**Silence**

Hommage aux Femmes Noires

Femme Noire, toujours présente tu as été, ouvrant la voie
Sans toi, là où je suis aujourd'hui je ne serais pas
Comment tu fais, je me demande,
Comment parviens-tu à tenir ?
Quand, à mon absence,
Rodent autour de toi plusieurs de mes frères

Violée, tu as été, ravagée, ton nom avili
Tu trouves encore la force d'être l'épine dorsale de notre race
Le pilier de notre race, notre cœur, notre fondement
Même lorsque enlevés et forcés, nous étions
A travailler à l'édification de la nation d'autrui

Lorsque d'Ankh,
Ils nous ont séparés pour nous donner leur croix
Ta foi en Dieu tu as su garder …Une foi que moi, j'ai perdue
En mon maître j'ai eu foi, je voulais qu'il me reçoive
Mais quand il devint le chef
Il me dit ne plus avoir besoin de moi
J'ai cru être seul, et personne pour m'accepter
Vers toi je me tournais, tu étais furieuse, mais ne me rejetais pas

Même quand ma colère je déversais sur toi
Femme Noire tu ne m'as jamais abandonné, ton amour absolu
J'ai compris que ce n'était pas toi,
Mais moi-même je détestais
Je ne savais tout simplement pas comment t'apprécier

Ma foi, j'ai retrouvée, Femme Noire ! La lumière, j'ai vue
J'ai compris que c'est toi dont
J'avais besoin et pas des blanches
Beaucoup sont juste curieuses de nous mettre dans leur lit
Tandis que tu es si divine que tu nous reçois les bras ouverts…
Et non les jambes ouvertes

D'un autre niveau tu es, si surréelle, si sublime
Les seuls rapports que je veux sont ceux avec ton esprit
Rien qu'à entendre ta voix,
D'un désir ardent mon corps est pris!
Parce qu'à ton âme je peux faire l'amour

Et ton corps vierge je préserve

Tu es ma future Femme Noire, je le sais
L'un à côté de l'autre,
De meilleurs moments nous avons en perspective

A Dieu j'ai demandé de me mettre sur la voie
Dieu, à ma porte t'envoya et en arrière je n'ai plus regardé
Des jours meilleurs sont à venir, certes je le perçois
Ainsi te dédier cet hommage est pour moi un honneur

Femme Noire, je regrette

Femme Noire, je regrette,
Pour toutes les privations,
Plus de cinq cents ans passés,
Et toujours, l'irrévérence
J'ai vraiment espoir
Que mes excuses acceptées
Pour tes attentes dont je n'ai pas été à la hauteur
Une force nous assaille,
En un mur dressé,
Elle nous oppresse
Pour que notre chute assurée
Notre échec est prévu
Parce qu'ils ont instauré le système,
Nous ne sommes plus à vendre,
Mais nos têtes sont toujours mises à prix
A leur image ils essaient de nous modeler
Pour nous réduire en charpie,
Mais tout leur contraire,
La famille est notre coeur
De la drogue, ils nous enivrent
Et la télé aussi
Leurs méthodes ils nous enseignent
Un lent génocide,
Ils se font hautains
Pour que nous perdions espoir
Avec condescendance ils nous traitent
Et rétorque que c'est une blague!
Femme noire, j'ai tenté!
Mais la lutte est rude
Joignons nos forces
La récompense est au bout
Nous apprenons encore une fois
A nous soutenir les uns les autres
A constituer la force
A vous, sœur et mère
Prière pardonnez-nous,
Sans relâche, nous implorons
Et je suis sur que nous y parviendrons
Ma sœur, je tenterai à mourir

Kendra

Chérie,
De mon ciel, tu es le soleil
Sur lequel flottent les rubans écarlates de notre amour
Qui, à l'image des anges d'ébène, enjambe la longévité
A travers les nuages stagnants
Tu es la charpente qui me soutient
A chaque fois que des montagnes je dois bouger

Vous qui de notre amour ne comprenez rien
Laissez-moi vous dire que quand loin d'elle je suis
Tout ce que je puis faire c'est d'avoir des visions
Pleines de merveilleux instants passés
A scruter l'âme de cette femme

Exit mes errements et pensées profondes sur
La manière dont nous passons les journées
A nous chuchoter à l'oreille de douces choses
Et révéler au monde entier
Que notre amour coule éternellement
Comme les chutes d'eau
Que poursuivent tous ceux qui sont en quête d'amour
Ignorant les rivières qui coulent
Et les lacs solitaires qui se lamentent,
Habitués qu'ils sont à la monotonie
Très jeunes, j'ai compris que seul l'idiot a soif
Lorsque l'eau coule en abondance
Alors sans hésiter, j'ai sauté dans les flots éternels de ton amour
Pour jouir du plaisir immense de voir ton sourire briller sur ma vie
Comme les éclatants rayons de soleil
Sur les parois mélancoliques de la lune

Chérie, de n'importe où du monde,
Je voyagerais en première classe
Juste pour te souhaiter à travers un baiser, une bonne nuit
Afin d'être la dernière image
En prélude à ton sommeil nocturne
Ainsi d'une volonté non altruiste
Tu m'accorderas partiellement une part dans tes rêves
Tandis qu'en toute sécurité,
Tu t'endormiras dans le lit de la fidélité

Bien que nous n'ayons pas encore enfanté
Me réveiller dans la sculpture ciselée de ta vie,
M'emplit d'opportunités
Je sais que des journées les plus épouvantables,
Je peux connaître
Tout autant que je peux rentrer me revigorer
Avec les douces sonorités de tes homélies

Chérie, en toute honnêteté
On m'a déjà dit être trop jeune pour le mariage
Ce conseil n'émanait que d'éphémères amoureux
Et puisque ces amours passagers ne sont
Que des ventouses de circonstance
Je jure de te vouer tout mon amour et non pas en partie

Chérie,
Je ne suis pas chrétien, mais en sécurité dans tes bras,
Je me sens renaître
Je ne suis pas bouddhiste, mais à tes cotés je sens en moi
l'illumination
Je ne suis pas musulman, mais je ressens le paradis en moi
Lorsque je pense à ton affection
Voilà pourquoi je n'ai pas hésité à épouser le premier
Et unique amour de ma vie
Même dans les moments difficiles
Je prie Luther tous les jours pour qu'il me rappelle
Ma préférence des pires moments à tes côtés
Aux bons temps auprès d'autre
Du passé à l'avenir, tout au long de ma de vie
Je ne vois rien d'autre
Que pure pensée positive de longues années
Auprès de mon épouse

Kendra, ma scintillante étoile
Mon ange africaine, pour toi mon amour impérissable
A l'ultime instant de ma vie, après mon dernier soupire
Saches qu'au septième ciel je serais,
Car tu as très haut porté mon âme
Jusqu'à ce jour t'honorer je continuerai car
Comme un patient Yuruba
Tu me combles
Ces mots j'écris pour que toi et le monde entier sachiez

181

Mon amour si profond que surréel
Tu es à l'image du fantasme qui mon esprit fait voguer
Comme des feuilles détachées des branches de ma poésie
Il est inimaginable que ces mots aient existés
Si Dieu ne t'avait créée
Créant ainsi la confiance qui nous a unit

Dans l'extase, prisonniers volontaires de notre amour mutuel
Cheminons chaque jour sur l'allée de la dévotion
A notre créateur et ancêtres
Rendons grâce pour avoir, deux âmes pures, fusionné

Other Products from Free Your Mind Publishing

<u>A Young Black Man's Anthem</u>

Omékongo's 1st spoken word CD!
Poetry in English, French, and Swahili!
Winner of the Cambridge Poetry Award for "Best CD"!
$15

<u>Signs of the Time</u>

Omékongo's 2nd spoken word CD!
Poetry in English, French, and Swahili!
Enhanced CD!
$15

Preview tracks at

www.omekongo.com

Quick Order Form

Fax orders: (617) 327-2840
Telephone orders: Call (617) 970-2439
Email orders: orders@omekongo.com
Postal orders: Free Your Mind Publishing, PO Box 70
Boston, MA 02131, USA

Please send the following books, disks or reports.

_____

_____

_____

Please send more FREE information on:
__ Other Products __ Speaking Engagements __Mailing Lists
__Consulting

Name: _____

Address: _____

City: _____ State: _____ Zip: _____

Telephone (day) _____

            (evening) _____

Email: _____
___ *Please add me to your e-mail mailing list!*

Sales tax: Add 7.75% sales tax for products shipped to
California addresses.

Shipping by air
U.S. $5.50 for first book, $4.50 for CD, and $2.50 for each
additional product.
International: $9.00 for first book or disk; $5.00 for each
additional product (estimate)

Payment: __Visa __Mastercard __Optima __AMEX __Discover

Card number: _____

Name on card: _____ Exp. Date: _____

"Opening eyes, one mind at a time."

FREE YOUR MIND
P U B L I S H I N G